Anticipating The Afterlife

A biblical exploration of why we die and what comes next

Anticipating The Afterlife

A biblical exploration of why we die and what comes next

Paul Luckraft

malcolm down
PUBLISHING

First published 2026 by Malcolm Down Publishing Ltd
www.malcolmdown.co.uk

29 28 27 26 7 6 5 4 3 2 1

British Library Cataloguing in Publication Data
A catalogue record for this book is available from the British Library.

ISBN 978-1-917455-61-9

Cover photo by Sarah Grace
Cover design by Esther Kotecha
Art direction by Sarah Grace

Printed in the UK

‘People are destined to die once,
and after that to face judgement.’

Hebrews 9:27

‘If someone dies, will they live again?’

Job 14:14

‘I am the resurrection and the life.
The one who believes in me will live,
even though they die.’

Jesus in John 11:25

‘Do not be afraid . . . I am the Living
One; I was dead, and now look,
I am alive for ever and ever!’

Jesus in Revelation 1:17-18

‘Then I saw “a new heaven
and a new earth”.’

Revelation 21:1

Endorsements

Paul Luckraft has added to his increasing collection of inspiring and informative books with another excellent publication, this time with a thematic approach to questions that concern all of us with regard to the afterlife. He writes with care, compassion and a strict precision as to what the Bible actually says.

Some may want to start by going straight to those chapters which intrigue them most, such as the sensitive chapters on the death of our pets and the sadness of the death of babies and children. Both of these matters stir our emotions and it is good to grasp what is the biblical truth. But in fact it is most profitable to read the book through from start to finish as interconnected lines of argument thread through the whole text. This is a book to treasure.

Revd Ian Farley, Rector, St John's, Buckhurst Hill.

Paul has produced a masterpiece of biblical exposition on the challenging and delicate matters which surround death and what comes afterwards. His book offers a comprehensive coverage of the whole topic at just the right depth so that it is informative without being overwhelming. Paul's style is very accessible which is particularly helpful in guiding us through the trickier concepts.

I learnt much from the way the early chapters address the key questions of what is death and what is life. The end of the book brings things together well, enabling us to apply and personalise what we have been reading.

Revd Canon John McGinley, leader of the Myriad church planting programme, author of *The Church of Tomorrow* and *Awaken*.

Confusion is woven through our world today and none more so than in the meaning of life, death and the afterlife. Courage is needed to blot out the multitude of contrasting opinions that swirl around us today, even within church circles.

As a Christian leader and teacher, Paul believes the only reliable source regarding the truth of our final destiny is God's Word, the Bible. That confidence is not simply based on an ancient script but supremely in the Word made flesh, Jesus Christ. Only Jesus has lived as a man, died, was buried and rose again, destroying the power of sin and death. As the Alpha and Omega, he alone has the first and the last word regarding our past, present and future.

This book is well researched and scholarly, and will make you think at a deep personal level. Underpinning it all is a pastoral and caring heart for each one of us. This becomes clear in the variety of questions Paul brings into play . . . what is death? . . . why do we die? . . . what about purgatory? . . . can we communicate with the dead and do they have a second chance? . . . what is heaven and hell? . . . and, of course, we must not forget the pet question, is there a 'doggy heaven'? as Paul puts it.

I found reading this book to be personally challenging and edifying but, above all, it left me with a greater desire for our eternal future with Christ to dictate and continually change the way I live today.

Mike Dwight, missionary, pastor and author of *Unbeliever to Overcomer.*

Who hasn't wondered what happens after death? For several months, Followers of the Way was honoured to listen to Paul's biblical exploration of the afterlife. Theologically grounded and well researched, our fellowship found his presentations both thought-provoking and challenging.

This side of eternity there are some things we will never know but, for Christians, assurance of the hereafter is vital, along with an understanding, no matter how incomplete, of what will happen not just to ourselves but to those we love. These questions, along with others, Paul unflinchingly addresses. Prepare to be challenged!

I warmly commend Paul's book to anyone who has ever wondered whether they can really trust God about life after death!

Lynda Rose, Anglican priest, writer, CEO of Voice for Justice UK, and leader of the online fellowship Followers of the Way.

Acknowledgements

Like all my previous books, this one started life as a series of short talks for my website, www.orchardseeds.com. The series can still be found there under the original title 'Aspects of the Afterlife'. Each talk became a chapter of this book and so, at times, the style of writing may reflect this. I would like to thank those who listened to the original talks and provided feedback.

In particular I want to express my gratitude to those from The Followers of the Way who heard me teach this material online. The discussion times at the end of each meeting were very helpful. I especially thank Lynda Rose for allowing me space in their schedule.

I am also grateful to those who read through earlier versions of the manuscript. Their insightful comments enabled me to make several significant improvements. My special thanks in this respect go to Ian Farley, John McGinley and Mike Dwight.

As always I am very grateful to those at Malcolm Down Publishing who have made this book possible. Special mention goes to my editor, Louise, for her usual prompt and efficient work, to Malcolm Down for his advice and expertise, and to Sarah Grace for providing the photograph which formed the basis for the front cover.

Finally I acknowledge those who have written on these issues before and have guided my own thinking. The following list includes the books I found most helpful.

Heaven	Randy Alcorn
The Great Unknown	Paul Blackham
40 Questions about Heaven and Hell	Alan W. Gomes
One Minute After You Die	Erwin W. Lutzer
A New Heaven and a New Earth	J. Richard Middleton
The Message of Heaven and Hell	Bruce Milne
What on Earth is Heaven?	James Paul
What I'm Looking Forward To: Life After Life After Death	David Pawson
Why We Die	Venky Ramakrishnan
Death and the Afterlife	Paul R. Williamson

Grudem's Systematic Theology

Vine's Expository Dictionary of Biblical Words

Contents

Chapter One

Introduction and Overview

In this book we tackle the often controversial and sensitive issue of human destiny, both for the individual as well as for humanity as a whole. What does lie ahead for each of us personally when our span of life on earth comes to an end? And what about humanity's ultimate fate? Is it one of extinction or renewal?

As you can imagine, there will be much to occupy our attention within this overall topic. There are many aspects of the afterlife for us to piece together, each of which will both demand and deserve careful investigation. Above all, we will need to be sure how much we *can* know compared to how much we might *want* to know.

Today's society may be secular and materialistic, and based largely upon humanism and rationalism, but surveys continue to show that a sizeable proportion of the population, both in the UK and elsewhere, still believe in some kind of afterlife. Despite a decline in traditional religious belief, many retain a hope that this life is not all there is.

A general summary of surveys undertaken would indicate that while around 25 per cent believe that at death we simply cease to exist, and another quarter prefer to remain agnostic, just over half still believe there is some kind of ongoing life after death. Of course, for some, maybe many, within this larger group, this may be no more than wishful thinking or, at best, a vague hope of something better to come. But even for those within this group who do have a firmer view of what might lie ahead, there is a great diversity of opinion. Perhaps not surprisingly, no single narrative emerges as to what an afterlife might be like.

For some, but perhaps not many, belief in an afterlife involves the concept of a regular life cycle, such as reincarnation or the transmigration of souls, a process in which we continually re-emerge in some kind of bodily form, a succession of rebirths designed to take us increasingly towards ultimate transcendence. Others think of the afterlife as a single journey away from this current life to a heavenly setting, never to return to anything remotely similar to what we have previously experienced. But even within this latter idea there is still a wide selection of views as to the nature of our final destination, ranging from a celestial resort where we can continue to indulge in what we have previously enjoyed on earth, to becoming some kind of angelic being, suitably attired, complete with halo and harp, ready to spend eternity in a new and very different state of existence.

Even if there is some kind of a heavenly afterlife, it is often assumed that everyone will be there. Or nearly everyone, as there may have to be some exceptions, a few extremely wicked people perhaps. But who would they be? And who gets to decide on the amount or type of wickedness that would result in exclusion from eternal bliss? My view might differ from yours. Indeed my view might be coloured by my own preferences of whom I would want to share eternity with!

Another common perception about a future heavenly existence is that it involves a place where one day we will all be reunited with our loved ones, something often stated at funerals to help sustain people in their loss. It is not surprising we seek such reassurance in times of extreme grief and sadness. We like to be told that our nearest and dearest are now looking down on us, and that all is peace and light. Overall, we have a keen natural desire for a story, any story, to end well, and that includes the big story of life. We want to know we will all live happily ever after, and hopefully not be too bored by the sameness of whatever the phrase 'for ever and ever' might entail.

But how much of all this is nothing more than hopeful optimism or utopian speculation? Can we determine any truth or reality within this huge diversity of opinions and confusing options? Should we even try? It is certainly tempting to say that we cannot come to any firm conclusions, so simply pick your own view and stick with that.

One reason why people assert we cannot know anything about the afterlife is that no-one has experienced death and come back to tell us about it or what to expect afterwards. It is also argued that the limitations of human knowledge and scientific investigations are such that we would need special revelation if we are ever to see beyond the veil into the afterlife, and that quite simply this we do not have.

However, Christians would disagree with both of these assertions. They claim that the Bible contains that special revelation, or at least as much as we can reasonably expect. Indeed they would say the Bible is the *only* reliable source of truth regarding our future destiny, the ultimate means of settling the great questions of the afterlife.

And then there is Jesus who was not only raised from the dead, but who then spent forty days presenting himself alive to his disciples with many proofs. He didn't merely teach about life after death, he experienced it, so his teaching both before and after his resurrection is critical to our thinking on these matters.

Of course, many may not accept the authority of either the Bible or of Jesus, but it is hoped they will at least give a fair hearing to what it, and he, says, and hence to what we offer in this book. An open and honest appraisal is all that can be asked for.

However, Christians must also be honest and realise that even with the Bible, we still cannot know everything. Believing that the Bible is reliable and truthful doesn't mean it tells us everything we would like to know. Some things are clearly set out, but in other areas the scriptures may have little to say. In some cases, mystery will persist or texts remain open to interpretation, so we must be humble and never claim to know more than we can.

There will be times when we can take what we know about God generally and apply this to some of our topics, but it is important not to attempt to be either too smart or over-spiritual in an attempt to make up for any perceived deficiency of the Bible. The worst option would be to fill in the gaps from elsewhere, from other more dubious sources. It is better to have unanswered questions than have answers that might be misleading.

So while this book is primarily for Christians who want greater assurance on what the Bible says, it is also intended to help those seeking to know what the Christian faith involves before deciding if they can commit to it. Some may be comforted by what we share in these pages, others may be disturbed, but hopefully everyone will be better informed as a result.

Our approach will be to examine what the Bible teaches and take in as much of the biblical data as we can. We make no claim to any special revelation on these matters, just a desire to accurately examine what we can know from the Bible. We will be as thorough as possible while recognising that certain matters will always be beyond our limited human comprehension. Much will remain a mystery. We can only leave these matters to faith, accepting that God alone has the final answers and retains the right to make all ultimate decisions. However, through a careful study of the scriptures we believe it is possible to discover certain truths that will reveal something about these important matters.

In particular, we will aim to combat errors and falsehoods that have arisen either through misunderstandings or speculation. We will draw our conclusions from biblical texts, interpreting them as accurately as possible, and within their context. We will provide certainty as far as we can but also admit that at times we either don't have a clue or cannot deduce much.

Before we begin, it may be useful to outline some of the main topics and questions that we will cover in this book, though not necessarily in this order.

One obvious factor to consider is what we mean precisely by death. In particular, what actually happens to us at the moment of death? Does any part of us survive? If so, what? What about our memories, our knowledge, our personality, our identity, gender and ethnicity?

Another important question is why do we die at all? Is it really necessary? Is there any purpose behind it, good or bad?

It is also fair to ask whether we will be able to recognise each other once we no longer have our current bodies. Indeed are we even conscious in any meaningful way, or is being dead best summed up by the term 'soul sleep'?

Then there is the matter of purgatory. Where did this idea come from and is there any truth in it?

Another key issue is that of communication with the dead, both us with them and them with us. Is it allowable? Or even possible?

Many will want to know what happens to their pets when they die. Is there an afterlife for animals, a sort of 'doggy heaven'? Might you one day be reunited with your favourite family pet or your well-loved animal companion?

Then there is the difficult subject of the death of babies and infants, which we will need to tackle with due sensitivity.

Another common question is whether our eternal destiny is fixed forever at death or whether we get a second chance.

Is there still an opportunity to repent and find salvation once you have died? This often goes under the theological title of Post-Mortem Evangelism.

We might also wonder what it was like for Jesus between his death and resurrection. Did he descend into hell as some creeds assert? If so, for what purpose, and what exactly was this 'hell'?

This leads on to the main issues of heaven and hell themselves. What should we think about both of these? And what about those who claim to have seen heaven, perhaps had what we call near-death experiences. How should we evaluate these?

Further major areas for consideration include judgement. How many are there in general, and what will judgement be like for Christians? Then there is the associated matter of rewards and punishments. For instance, are there different degrees of both?

Then there is the great and glorious theme of the resurrection of the body, but which in itself raises many questions. For instance, how many different resurrections does the Bible describe, and what can we learn in advance about the new body we will have?

So overall there is much to explore. There is no doubt that it will be a challenging task to bring clarity into the midst of all the uncertainty and conflicting views. But let's start with the one thing everyone is absolutely 100 per cent agreed upon, the certainty of death itself.

Chapter Two

The Certainty of Death

In this chapter we will be focusing on death itself and our attitudes towards it. Death features a great deal in the entertainment industry (TV, film, theatre and, of course, the many murder mystery and crime novels), yet its reality isn't something we choose to talk about very often. This may not be totally surprising, given that it seems to represent the end of everything we know and love. Mention it if necessary but otherwise can we please change the topic and find something more pleasant to talk about? Yet avoiding discussing death altogether can leave us vulnerable and unprepared. We always make the necessary preparations for any significant journey. We would be foolish not to. So when it comes to that great journey beyond death into the afterlife, an understanding of what is to come is especially necessary given that nothing is more certain for every one of us.

Most people are familiar with the famous quote that the only certain things in life are death and taxes. This saying is usually attributed to Benjamin Franklin, one of the founding fathers of the United States and one of those who drafted and signed the Declaration of Independence. In a letter of 1789 to Jean-Baptiste Le Roy, he wrote: 'Our new Constitution is now established, and has an appearance that promises permanency; but in this world nothing can be said to be certain, except death and taxes.' However, Franklin was not the first to use this phrase, which appears earlier in a work by Daniel Defoe entitled *The Political History of the Devil* in which he wrote, 'Things as certain as death and taxes, can be more firmly believed.' But even this may not be the origin of the phrase as the line 'Tis impossible to be sure of anything but Death and Taxes' appears in a comedy play entitled *The Cobbler of Preston* by Christopher Bullock, published in 1716.

While we are in a literary mode we might also take a moment to smile over Margaret Mitchell's take on the matter. In her novel *Gone with the Wind*, one of her characters states, 'Death, taxes and childbirth! There's never any convenient time for any of them.'

The point is an obvious one. Death happens to us all. And globally it occurs at a startling rate. There is a fascinating website called Worldometer. (If you put this into your search engine you might be directed to worldometers.info, though other similar websites are available.) Here you will discover real-time counters displaying up-to-date statistics for diverse topics such as world population, economics, the environment, energy, health and much more. Watching the numbers tick over is engrossing and often quite scary, especially those that reflect the world's population. Doing some basic calculations from these ever-changing metrics we discover there are over 170,000 deaths a day worldwide. This equates to about 2 every second, so while you are reading this chapter about 1,800 people will draw their last breath. Overall, this totals over 62 million every year, nearly the equivalent of the entire UK population.

This seems an alarming amount. Just watch the second hand of a clock tick along and count for yourself the deaths that are occurring. But let's not forget there are 8.2 billion people on the planet, which puts such figures into some kind of context. In addition, while you are reading this chapter, some 3,800 people will be born, which is also a staggering figure to take in. Just over 4 per second will take their first breath. That's a net gain of 187,000 per day, hence the continual rapid rise in the world's population. All these new people coming to planet earth. Where are they coming from? And all these people leaving our world. Where are they going? Here are some big questions, at a global level.

But death is not only universal, it is also intensely personal. Death may be common to the whole human race, yet each individual faces their own death alone. No one else can endure it for us, or take our place. Others may be present, providing comfort and support, but only the one dying can go through that final moment, isolated and unaccompanied on their final journey.

In addition, our death will be an experience which we will never have encountered before. It is a one-off. Nor can there be an opportunity for any kind of practice run or rehearsal. Inevitably this can create a sense of fear or nervousness. What does lie beyond? What will this really mean for me? Such questions naturally make us anxious.

People face up to this moment in different ways. For some there is a sense of helplessness and resignation; for others, an awareness of peace. But for many it is the most terrifying event imaginable, one best confronted with denial or anger. They would echo the words of the poet Dylan Thomas: 'Do not go gentle into that good night; Rage, rage against the dying of the light.'

Some may try and deflect their feelings about death through humour. One such was the comedian Woody Allen. In a one-act play from 1975, appropriately called *Death*, he quipped: *'It's not that I'm afraid to die. I just don't want to be there when it happens.'*

He also verbalised a sentiment which many might adhere to when he said, 'I don't want to achieve immortality through my work; I want to achieve immortality through not dying. I don't want to live on in the hearts of my countrymen; I want to live on in my apartment.'

Yet the fact remains that even if we accept that we ourselves will one day be gone from this earth, we still have a strong desire to be remembered in some way.

Naturally, we all try and stay alive for as long as possible. We instinctively avoid what might result in our death, such as accidents, enemies and disease. Moreover, we somehow manage not to live in constant fear of death or complete dread of our own mortality. Most of us appear, at least on the surface, to be able to go through life without letting our future demise affect us too deeply on a day-to-day basis. Some people by nature are more laid back, with a 'whatever will be, will be' attitude. Let's just take each day as it comes. Eat, drink and be merry, for tomorrow we die, where hopefully tomorrow isn't actually the day after today. Others are inherently more forward looking and so the inevitable end of their life features more regularly in their thinking.

But wherever we are on this spectrum, one day we *will* run out of life. We may find it easy to persuade ourselves that the figure quoted earlier of 170,000 deaths per day always refers to other people, but the fact remains that tomorrow you could be included in that statistic. To act and think as though death is what occurs to someone else and will never happen to me is to live unrealistically.

Depressing as it may seem, the philosopher Heidegger, in his book *Being and Time*, stated the obvious when he said that 'as soon as man comes to life he is at once old enough to die'. We have to live authentically in the face of death. We cannot pretend it will never happen. Somehow we have to find a way to live in anticipation rather than denial.

The knowledge that we will someday die will inevitably, in one way or another, shape our journey through life. Death may come tomorrow or decades hence but its prospect casts a shadow over the whole of our lives. The certainty of death forces us to evaluate our worldview, and brings to the surface our deepest convictions about this world and about ourselves. In particular it brings the greater questions of existence to the fore, questions about the nature of reality and the world around us. What is life? What does it mean to be human? Do we sense that somehow we must be more than merely the dust of the earth? Does the fact that we will die create a hope that life is larger than the boundaries of terrestrial existence, that death is not the end, indeed cannot be the end.

Some, however, may still consider it a waste of time to think about the afterlife. They argue that life's too short to spend time brooding about such things! I just want to get through this day and the next!

For others the main impetus in life is simply to enjoy what they have in front of them now and not think too deeply about what is to come. They find other, more immediate, things to occupy their attention, such as the latest edition of their favourite TV programme or the current form of their favoured football team. They might agree with Bill Shankly, the legendary former manager of Liverpool Football Club, who on interview is recorded as saying, 'Some people think football is a matter of life and death. I assure you, it's much more important than that.' Well, yes, ok . . . Enjoy your football, or whatever your passion is, but one day you will need to think that something does matter more.

How we live now is often largely influenced by what we believe about the life beyond. This remains the case even if we deny there is any form of afterlife at all. Such beliefs, or lack of them, direct our energies and determine how we spend our time now. This is seen not only in the practicalities of life but also in our philosophy of life, including our attitude to others and towards God.

Christians are, or at least should be, committed to the idea of a glorious life beyond death. The New Testament is consistently orientated towards such a hope. The Christian mindset should therefore cultivate an eternal perspective as part of living by faith in the course of everyday life in this world. For the Christian, death is different. It *has* to be different now that Jesus has conquered death. Death *has* lost its sting. And we should steadfastly believe this.

But as well as faith it can help to have some assured facts, and so our purpose here is to sift for biblical truth in these matters, not merely to satisfy curiosity but also to enhance confidence. The greater the assurance you have, the more likely you are to be an overcomer when the going gets tough or when facing persecution and the possibility of an imminent death at the hands of others.

Really knowing what we believe also helps us when we talk to those not yet in the Christian faith. If *we* don't know what is going to happen, then what can we say to others? Unfortunately there is a lot of what has been called Christian mythology or folklore on the matter of life after death, much of which has taken the place of what Christians should actually believe. It is important not to encourage people to believe in the equivalent of spiritual fairy-tales or even in half-truths. For instance, what do we really mean by saying that our ultimate destiny is to 'die and go to heaven'? This over-simplistic statement may be comforting but it only begs more questions and, let's face it, the way the church has often portrayed heaven is not necessarily that attractive to unbelievers. We need the strongest possible message about the afterlife when it comes to preaching the gospel so that those who put their trust in God's love and mercy, and his saving work through Jesus, can cherish what is to come.

The writer to the Hebrews reminds us that 'people are destined to die once', adding 'and after that to face judgement' (Heb. 9:27). Perhaps it is the prospect of facing judgement that causes many to fear death or deny any afterlife. They prefer instead to 'imagine there's no heaven', and 'no hell below us'. But that is no solution. We must live with eternity in view.

'After that . . . judgement'. But there are many more things that come after death than judgement, and we will be looking at these later. But before all this, we will start to grapple with another mysterious and complex topic, that of life before death.

Chapter Three

Life Before Death: The Nature of Man

Before we discuss the various issues of life after death we ought to turn our attention to the matter of life *before* death. In particular, what exactly do we mean by 'life', and what is the nature of man (and woman) that enables us to experience life in the way we do?

All the features of the afterlife, which we will be exploring in this book, have their own complexities and open up a multiplicity of complications which require careful investigation. The same is true of the matter of life before death and the inherent nature of human beings. However, one thing beyond dispute is that if you are reading this book then you are most definitely alive. You are a living being. Moreover, you don't just have *a life*, you have *Life*. Life itself. But where did this 'Life' come from? Having an answer to this may give us a clue as to how our life ends and what may come next.

The debate about the origin of life in general, and of humankind in particular, has become highly contentious, with many views competing for our attention. Our approach, as we said before, is to look for answers within the biblical text and so we must consider what God has told us in the opening book of the Bible, Genesis. For many, the first chapters of Genesis are problematic, even a source of great dispute. But whether you consider that the Genesis account about Adam and Eve is historically accurate in all its details, or that it is merely a story conveying certain truths, does not matter so much in this case. What does matter is that you accept that what is revealed there is indeed truth. Only then can these verses provide us with meaningful insights into the origin and nature of humankind.

The key verse is Genesis 2:7, where having taken dust from the ground to create the physical part of man (his body), God then breathed into that first man (Adam) and he became a 'living being'. In Hebrew, this is *nefesh chaya*. The second word, *chaya*, relates to the Hebrew word for life, whereas *nefesh* has been variously translated as 'creature' or 'person', or even, quite commonly, 'soul'. Before we dig deeper into this important word regarding the nature of man, it is worth noting that the same phrase, *nefesh chaya,* is also used earlier in Genesis to refer to other living creatures. For instance, in Genesis chapter 1 verses 20 and 21, the water is filled with 'living creatures', and in verse 24 the land brings forth all kinds of 'living creatures'. In all these verses, the same phrase, *nefesh chaya,* is used, so this is not unique to man. However, where there *is* a significant difference is in the origin of that *nefesh*, in that man received his *nefesh* directly from God, through the breath of God, whereas for other creatures this was not the case, though exactly how it happened is not recorded.

Another point worth noting about Genesis 2:7 is that the phrase for the breath of life (which God breathed into the nostrils of the first man) is *nishmat chayim*, rather than the more expected *ruach chayim*. (*Ruach* is the more usual word for breath, and can also mean wind or spirit, whereas *nishmat* relates to *neshamah*, the more normal kind of breathing which largely goes unnoticed as we don't hear it.) The phrase *ruach chayim* does, however, appear later in Genesis to refer to creatures which have the breath of life in them. We find this, for instance, in Genesis 6:17, 7:15, 7:22, where the meaning of the phrase could be expanded to suggest 'the breath of the spirit of life' or 'the breath that is the spirit of life'. However, because *ruach* can mean breath as well as spirit, the use of the phrase *ruach chayim* in these verses may simply be referring to creatures that need to breathe in order to maintain the life within them, rather than anything that we might think of as 'spiritual'.

But what is most important for us to recognise at this point is that in Genesis 2:7 it is *God* who breathed into Adam. It is this which makes man unique and hence different from the animals. It is part of being made in the image and likeness of God (Gen. 1:26-27). Animals may also have a *nefesh* but it is of a different, lower kind, which means they don't have the capacity to survive the death of the body as we do, something we will discuss further in a later chapter.

As we have seen, Genesis 2:7 does not contain the word *ruach* or spirit so although our *nefesh* is created by the breath of God, we must beware of inferring that at this initial moment of creation God somehow placed his Spirit in man (Adam) or indeed that man was created with a separate 'spiritual' component.

There is inevitably something of a mystery about the initial creation of humankind, but there are two things we can assert from the biblical text. One is that God didn't take an existing living being and enhance it, or upgrade it, by adding a 'spirit'. The other is that neither did he create Adam as a spirit and then place this inside a body. Rather he first created a body and then animated it via his breath. This means there never was a moment when Adam existed without a body and the same can be said of every human being. Certain Greek philosophies teach that we all pre-exist as souls in heaven, waiting to be incarnated into this world at some point in time. But the Bible maintains that each individual is created in the womb as a physical being which becomes a whole person, a living being, though again there is mystery to all this!

Some may still argue that there is a distinct part in each of us which we can refer to as 'spirit' and we will take this up in the next chapter. It is certainly true that we have abilities different from the animals which we might categorise as spiritual, such as worship, prayer and fellowship with God. But we also use our mind, our emotions and our body in such activities. Our spiritual life is based upon our whole being and not restricted to a distinct element which we might call 'spirit'. We will consider more about *ruach*, or spirit, in due course, but meanwhile let us see what more we can learn about *nefesh*.

The word *nefesh* occurs about 780 times in the Old Testament and relates to the verbal form *napash*, which refers to the act of breathing or taking in breath. There is no single English equivalent of what *nefesh* represents in Hebrew, which makes it difficult to pin down that precisely.

By some counts there are nearly 30 different English words used in translation. What they do have in common is that they refer in some way to the non-physical side of life. Examples include words such as 'person', 'being' and 'heart'. These all feature quite regularly, but the most common translation of *nefesh* is 'soul' which occurs over 400 times. This may make sense in most passages but not in others where it must be translated differently. For example, in Leviticus 17:11, the *life* of a creature is in the blood is better than the *soul* is in the blood.

Translating *nefesh* as 'person' is also more appropriate in some places. For instance, Genesis 46:26 refers to the 66 *nefesh* or people who went down to Egypt with Jacob. These were living persons, and so should be translated as such. We also occasionally find that *nefesh* is used to refer to a dead person, where again we should expect the translation to make this clear (see Lev. 21:11; Num. 6:6).

Another use of *nefesh* is as the equivalent of a personal pronoun such as 'I' or 'me' or 'my'. In which case, 'my soul' simply means 'me' or 'myself'. For instance, the psalmist may say, 'Bless the Lord, O my soul', or, 'Praise the Lord, my soul' (see Psalms 103, 104, 146). In these cases, the psalmist is not addressing his soul as though it is independent of himself, nor is he telling just part of himself to do something. He does not regard his soul as something distinct from him or which has a life of its own. Rather he is saying 'all that is within me' or 'all that I am' should engage in praising the Lord.

It is often suggested we should think of *nefesh* as the vitalising life force for the body and hence for the person as a whole. It is what invigorates and energises us, and makes us fully alive as a human being. All this seems reasonable, provided we don't then conclude that our bodies are simply the means of accommodating or housing our soul, a somewhat secondary role for the physical part of us.

In scripture a person is always seen holistically as a single individual entity. Your soul isn't something you possess as an element within. It describes you in totality. Overall, the biblical view of man is that he is an animated body rather than an incarnated soul. In short, we do not *have* souls, we *are* souls. We *live as* souls. We also use the word in this way when we send out the distress signal SOS. 'Save our souls' is not a call for eternal salvation, but a cry to be rescued from our current danger. Get me, all of me, out of this alive!

Overall, we can conclude so far that while living on earth each one of us is formed from a union of two components: a material substance (dust from the ground) and an immaterial substance (the breath of life given to us by God). The result is that we are a living soul, a term which expresses a man's total nature, or his person. In simple terms, a human being consists of a physical part and a non-physical part, which we could equally refer to as a visible part and an invisible part.

As already indicated, animals also have *nefesh* but not of that higher enhanced kind which humans have been supplied by God. So animals are not persons as we are. They are just living, breathing creatures. However, the fact they are described as having *nefesh* is what sets them apart from plants, trees and inanimate objects generally. But, to stress again, our *nefesh* is different from that of the animals. Ours is a God-breathed *nefesh* which distinguishes us from all other creatures and gives us the possibility of eternal life with our creator.

What we have said so far concerns what we are like as humans while alive on earth. But what about after death, which is, after all, our main study? What exactly is death and what happens when we die?

The best single-word description of death is separation. At the moment of death, you become cut off from all other people on earth and all you have known in this world. But you leave one thing behind. You don't take your body with you. Nor does it disappear immediately. It remains, which is why we refer to it as 'your remains' or 'your mortal remains'. But it is now 'life*less*'. It is still a body but the person has gone. All that is left is what we call a corpse. The non-physical part is no longer there. It has been separated from the physical part, almost the reverse of what happened when Adam was created, and so what remains appears to us as without life just as Adam would have been before God breathed into his body.

The well-known marching song from the American Civil War tells us that 'John Brown's body lies a-mouldering in the grave, but his soul goes marching on'. Is this an accurate description of death and its aftermath? The body in one place, the soul travelling on to another? Some may prefer to talk, or sing, about his spirit marching on, not his soul. They may argue that this is a more biblical scenario. We will pick this up in the next chapter so perhaps, before we finish this chapter, we should say something about the word 'spirit' (*ruach*).

In biblical Hebrew the word *ruach* occurs 378 times. As often with Hebrew words, it has several meanings and can be translated in various ways. The most common is 'spirit' (around 240 times) but it can also mean breath (or even air for breathing) and wind (something Jesus makes use of when speaking to Nicodemus in John chapter 3). In all these cases the emphasis is on something invisible or intangible, so perhaps after all, *ruach* is a better way of describing the non-physical part of man, the part which survives death.

Certain biblical texts seem to support this. Ecclesiastes, in his usual questioning manner, at one point ponders if the human spirit rises upward after death, rather than down into the earth (Eccl. 3:21). Later he is more assertive that 'the dust returns to the ground it came from, and the spirit returns to God who gave it' (Eccl. 12:7).

In the New Testament, James writes that 'as the body without the spirit is dead, so faith without deeds is dead' (Jas 2:26). Then there is the example of Jesus on the cross. Just before he breathes his last, he cries out, 'Father, into your hands I commit my spirit' (Luke 23:46). And then in John's gospel, just after Jesus declared, 'It is finished', we read that 'he bowed his head and gave up his spirit' (John 19:30).

In Acts, Stephen prays in a similar fashion while being stoned to death, 'Lord Jesus, receive my spirit' (Acts 7:59). All this is reminiscent of Psalm 31:5, where David says, 'Into your hands I commit my spirit,' though here the context is less likely to be pre-death and may just reflect David generally saying to God, 'I give myself to you,' as he looks for deliverance from a difficult situation in life.

So overall, there does seem to be enough biblical evidence to claim that at death it is the spirit, not the soul, which leaves the body. So now we have a dilemma. After death do we survive as a soul or a spirit? Which word should we use? Is there a significant difference between them? And does this mean that during our earthly life we should talk about having a soul *and* a spirit as well as a body? We will pick this up in our next chapter.

Chapter Four

The Nature of Man: Body, Soul and Spirit?

We ended the last chapter by asking whether we should think of ourselves as body and soul, or body and spirit, or even as body, soul and spirit. There are varying views on this which we will investigate carefully by considering what the scripture offers on this debate, all the while focusing on our main area of concern, namely what happens to us beyond death.

Before we look at the main debate as to whether man is in two parts (bipartite) or three (tripartite) we should mention there are some who believe there is only one element to a human being, namely the physical body. This view, called monism, argues that the body is the whole person and that there is no non-physical part distinct from the body. Words such as 'soul' or 'spirit' are just alternative expressions for the physical person rather than anything extra to the body. But this would mean that nothing survives death at all, which rules it out from a biblical perspective.

Moreover, this is not a typical view. Nearly everyone, including those without any specific Christian faith or understanding, accepts that there seems to be a non-physical part to man, usually called a soul. But beyond this basic acceptance, further consensus on what makes up this non-physical part is hard to pin down.

The most popular idea is that we are a tripartite being, made up of body, soul and spirit. This has widespread appeal and is commonly taught in evangelical circles. However, as we shall see, this is difficult to fully sustain biblically and is not generally upheld in the more academic world. One justification used to support the idea that we are tripartite is that God is a trinity and so we, being made in his image, must somehow reflect this in a tri-unity of our own. But this is a rather spurious argument and by no means conclusive.

If we are a tripartite being, with a soul and a spirit as separate entities, then we should be able to say how each of these parts functions independently. The usual theory is that the soul is also divided into three parts, namely the mind, the emotions and the will. And so it is with our soul that we think, feel and make decisions. As for our spirit, it is then claimed that this part of us directly relates to God. It is here we can experience God and communicate with him. A man's spirit is thus a higher faculty that comes alive when we are 'born again'. Then we are able to pray to God and worship him. It is further maintained that it is within our spirit that the Holy Spirit resides, and it is from there that he rules in the life of a believer.

However, this distinction between soul and spirit, and what each part does, is somewhat artificial, even forced. We have seen earlier that both the Old and the New Testaments have distinct words for soul and spirit: *nefesh* and *ruach* in Hebrew, *psuche* and *pneuma* in Greek. But the problem is that their usage is not uniform. These words for soul and spirit, whether in Hebrew or in Greek, are often used interchangeably or in parallel, and in such a way that functionally they are not so easily distinguishable. The spirit often duplicates the soul's supposed role within the human person, and vice versa. Here are some biblical texts to illustrate this.

Firstly in John's gospel, regarding the death of Lazarus and the sorrow this was causing, we read that Jesus was 'deeply moved in *spirit* and troubled' (John 11:33). But later, in John 12:27, concerning his own imminent death, Jesus says 'my *soul* is troubled'. And then in John 13:21, regarding his betrayal, we are back to Jesus being 'troubled in *spirit*' (italics in these illustrations mine). It seems from these examples that the words for soul and spirit are interchangeable, as there is no indication of any particular distinction in how Jesus was inwardly troubled on these separate occasions.

Then, in Luke 1:46-47, as part of what has become known as the Magnificat, Mary declares, 'My soul glorifies the Lord and my spirit rejoices in God my Saviour.' It is unlikely that one part of Mary is glorifying God while another part of her is rejoicing in him. Rather, here we have a typical example of Hebrew parallelism where the change of word does not indicate two distinct activities but, through repetition, is reinforcing the same thing. Also in this passage we see that the soul is engaging in an activity we might think of as 'spiritual'. Whether translated as glorifying or magnifying or praising the Lord, this is something we might expect to be reserved solely for the spirit.

Then there are reverse examples where the spirit is involved in thinking or knowing something, which is usually assumed to be an activity of the mind and so part of what the soul does. For example, in Mark 2:8 'Jesus knew in his spirit that this was what they [the teachers of the law] were thinking'. Then in 1 Corinthians 2:11 Paul states, 'For who knows a person's thoughts except their own spirit within them?' We might wonder why there is no mention of the soul in such verses.

Equally, reference is made elsewhere to the body and the spirit but not to the soul. For instance, in 2 Corinthians 7:1 we are told to 'purify ourselves from everything that contaminates body and spirit'. Should we not also avoid contaminating our soul? And in 1 Corinthians 7:34 we read that an unmarried woman can be 'devoted to the Lord in body and spirit'. Should not her soul also show devotion?

There is also the well-known observation in James 2:26 that 'the body without the spirit is dead'. But this leads to the question as to whether the body without the soul isn't equally dead.

The point we are making in all this is that the distinction between soul and spirit is not as clear cut in scripture as we would like it to be, especially if we want to uphold the tripartite view which distinguishes between them and which is often summarised by saying that each person *is* a spirit, *has* a soul, and *lives within* a body.

It could be argued that the texts we have been considering above have all been about life before death. What about life after death? Do we find anything more conclusive there? Not really.

In Matthew 10:28 Jesus says, 'Do not be afraid of those who kill the body but cannot kill the soul. Rather, be afraid of the One who can destroy both soul and body in hell.' There is no mention of spirit here.

In 1 Corinthians 5:5 Paul, dealing with a matter of gross immorality in the church, says that they should 'hand this man over to Satan for the destruction of the flesh, so that his spirit may be saved on the day of the Lord'. But there is no mention of what might happen to his soul.

Some texts do clearly refer to the *spirits* of those who have departed. For instance, Hebrews 12:23 mentions 'the spirits of the righteous made perfect', presumably in heaven, and in 1 Peter 3:19 we read that Jesus 'made proclamation to the imprisoned spirits', though it doesn't say exactly who they are or where they are imprisoned. We will look at this strange little passage again in a later chapter.

But then, just in case we think this is definitive, the book of Revelation twice mentions that John, in his heavenly vision, saw the *souls* of those slain because of the word of God and the testimony they maintained about Jesus (Rev. 6:9, 20:4).

So we seem to be going round in circles, or at least back and forth. In particular, the biblical writers do not seem to mind whether they say a soul or spirit has departed, as though both mean the same thing, and that either one of these words can represent the continuing existence of the original person in the life beyond death.

Moreover, it is particularly telling that nowhere in the Bible do we find the joint phrase 'soul and spirit' to refer to a departed person. If the tripartite nature of man is correct we might expect to find this phrase somewhere, if only to reassure us that both soul and spirit survive together, that neither of these is missing in the afterlife.

Overall, it has proved difficult to define precisely any complete distinction between soul and spirit because their functions at least overlap, if not fully coincide. Moreover, we should add that the body is usually also involved in whatever the soul or spirit does. Whether we are thinking, feeling, deciding, praying, worshipping and so on, we cannot do any of these without our body. In every case our brain and nervous system is involved, as will often be much of the rest of our body. So regardless of whether we think of ourselves as being in two parts or three, we should always take a holistic approach, especially as the Bible invariably emphasises the overall unity of a human being, a unity created by God in the beginning.

If the argument for a tripartite view of man is not conclusive, maybe the bipartite idea is more sustainable. In which case, we still have to accommodate two distinct words for soul and spirit. One approach is simply to be content with referring to the two parts as physical and non-physical, with the latter being thought of jointly as 'soul-spirit' or maybe as a 'spiritual soul'. This maintains a unity within the non-physical part and thus avoiding too sharp a distinction which scripture does not allow for. It also agrees with what we discovered in our last chapter when we saw in Genesis 2:7 how God created us as a living being, *nefesh chaya*, a God-breathed *nefesh* within a material body.

We can draw all this to a conclusion as follows. While alive on earth we are a two-part person: a material body and a soul-spirit. At death these two parts separate. Once the soul-spirit departs, the body can no longer survive. It remains as a corpse. You still exist as a person but now in one part, just your soul-spirit which continues to function with regards to personhood. It is this which carries into the afterlife all that made you the person you are, including your life memories, personality and self-consciousness. At death these survive because they are lodged within your soul-spirit. Thus, in the intermediate state of the afterlife (that is before being resurrected in a new body), you will still be known as you, both by yourself and by others.

We saw in the last chapter the flexibility of the word 'soul' which can also mean 'person', so we can continue to use this word both before death (to describe the embodied soul-spirit) and after death (to refer to the disembodied soul-spirit) as in both of these circumstances you are a person. Effectively, the word 'soul' acts as an abbreviation for the whole person whether in a physical body or not.

Does all this help resolve the issues discussed? Only you can decide. It does seem to fit most scriptures, though some would argue not all, and so we end this chapter with those texts which for some people still suggest we are tripartite in the traditional sense.

In 1 Thessalonians 5:23 Paul says, 'May your whole spirit, soul and body be kept blameless at the coming of our Lord Jesus Christ.' Isn't this proof we are in three distinct parts? Not necessarily. Paul is not here issuing a doctrinal statement or discussing the nature of man. He is ending his letter with a blessing upon the believers in Thessalonica, using the phrase 'whole spirit, soul and body' not to distinguish between them but to indicate the totality of our being. This is similar to when Jesus was asked about the greatest commandment. He replied, 'Love the Lord your God with all your heart and with all your soul and with all your mind and with all your strength' (Mark 12:30, based upon Deut. 6:5, cf Matt. 22:37). No-one suggests that here Jesus is defining man to be in four parts (or maybe five, if we include 'spirit' which is not mentioned here). Rather it means every bit of us, as a whole. Love God with everything you've got. Equally, Paul, at the end of 1 Thessalonians, is not listing different parts for the purposes of distinction, but piling them up for emphasis. May you be kept totally blameless in every way.

Then, in Hebrews 4:12 we read, 'For the word of God is alive and active. Sharper than any double-edged sword, it penetrates even to dividing soul and spirit . . .' Does this indicate we have two distinct parts within our body? On the face of it this is a strange concept anyway. Why would God want to separate the soul from the spirit? What would such division achieve? But, as in 1 Thessalonians 5:23, this is also not a doctrinal statement about the nature of man. Rather it is an illustration of the power of the Word of God, that it can get into every part of us. The context is that of judging us and exposing what we are like deep within. The point being made is that we can't hide from the searching power of God's word. Even in our inmost being, God knows what we are really like. So here the phrase 'soul and spirit' is not defining distinct parts but creating an impression about the power of God's word. Some even suggest this is a case of hyperbole, a literary form involving exaggeration, and that we should read the verse as saying that the soul and the spirit are actually indivisible, but that if it were possible to separate them, then the word of God could do so, such is its power.

In this chapter we have debated a complex matter, and some may have found it unsatisfactory or less than persuasive, but it has been necessary and hopefully helpful for what will come later in the book.

Chapter Five

Why Do We Die?

We have commented earlier in this book on the certainty of death, which is obviously true from an observational standpoint, but we could still ask what is it that makes death so certain. Why *do* we all die? In this chapter we will look at this question under two main headings: biological and theological.

Have you ever wondered what will be the actual cause of *your* death? If you were to make a list you would presumably include illness and disease, as well as what is termed 'old age', meaning the natural decay of the body as it wears out. Other possible reasons for your demise are accidents and disasters of many kinds. You could be killed by someone else, intentionally or otherwise. You may even die in war or due to an act of terrorism. The list seems depressingly long. But the basic reason is that in some way your body ceases to function in the way it has been doing, often over many years.

In simple terms, the most common understanding is that death occurs when our heart stops beating or our lungs cease to breathe. We thus think of the moment of death to be when we draw our last breath or the final time our heart takes a beat. But actually, even after this has happened some functions of the body do continue for a while. For instance, the liver goes on trying to get rid of any alcohol in the system, and various enzymes and bacteria in the gut still go on operating. In fact, at the point we call death most cells in our body are still alive. It takes time for them individually to stop 'breathing' or functioning. So even if one essential part of our body ceases to operate, it can take a while for everything else to shut down.

It is also well known that individually cells die all the time with no overall adverse effects or threats to our whole body. Indeed, it is often thought that cells in the human body replace themselves every seven years, suggesting that over time you become an entirely new physical being. This is not strictly true, however, as not all cells regenerate at the same rate. Some, such as blood and skin cells, thankfully replace themselves rapidly. Others take more time. For instance, those of the liver and the heart. Indeed only about 40 per cent of the cells in the heart are replaced over a whole lifetime, and brain cells are renewed at the very slow rate of about 2 per cent each year.

Nevertheless, it is true that at the cellular level parts of us are dying all the time. In particular, some cells have to die in order for new ones to take their place and so allow the body to grow and develop. This is specifically so in a baby, where certain cells are programmed to die to pave the way for those of an adult. This biological process of cell death is called apoptosis, should you want to find out more.

It has been said that over a lifetime we die gradually and then suddenly. We can definitely cope with certain parts of us dying in some way without this being totally life-threatening, but eventually there comes a critical moment when we can no longer function as a coherent organic whole. At this point there is a system-wide failure and death results.

Overall, the main route to death still remains that of getting old. This may be accompanied by disease or other problems which might get worse as we get older. However, 'old age' still features regularly as the cause of death on a death certificate, even if accompanied by one or more other contributing factors. Ageing is clearly a key element that leads towards the death of the body, so what exactly is ageing and why is it inevitable?

Ageing itself is usually seen as a gradual process involving many small steps or defects. At first the body can easily overcome these but, over time, they become more and more significant, and ultimately serious. From a medical perspective, ageing has been described as the accumulation of issues at the molecular, genetic and cellular level which build up until they exceed our ability to repair them. This may or may not be an accurate description of what happens as we get older, but we certainly do our best to escape the ageing process, perhaps hoping this will somehow postpone or even cancel death. In recent times there has been a large increase in the amount of money spent on anti-ageing products and processes in a desperate attempt to stay young. But however rich you are, the elixir of youth remains elusive.

There has also been a great deal of investment in scientific projects aimed at reversing the ageing process and also in the new science, some would say pseudoscience, of cryonics, where the body is frozen at death. People pay tens of thousands of pounds to have their dead body preserved at extremely low temperatures, in the anticipation that it can be revived in the future when medical science has progressed enough to heal the currently incurable disease that led to their death, or even to reverse death itself.

In some ways it can still be difficult to decide exactly when death takes place or whether it has actually occurred. The lack of a pulse or evidence of breathing is not always decisive. Cardiac arrest can be reversed by CPR (cardiopulmonary resuscitation), a procedure used when someone's heartbeat or breathing has stopped. This involves repeated chest compressions and mouth-to-mouth rescue breaths. Nowadays, brain death is often regarded as an accurate indicator of death, but even here there is some debate over whether it is possible to be entirely sure over the complete loss of brain function.

It is interesting that even at the crucifixion of Jesus it wasn't totally clear to the Romans that he had died until they plunged a spear into his side (John 19:34). This would have ruptured the pericardial sac and the pleural cavities. The resulting sudden flow of blood and water exiting his body together (something now known as pericardial effusion) confirmed to them that death had indeed taken place.

Mainly, however, death is instantly recognisable. A corpse generally looks as though the essence of life has left, and a pallor to the skin often develops soon after death as blood drains from the capillaries near the body's surface. Of course, in some murder mysteries (spoiler alert!) the plot twist may revolve around someone faking their own death, fooling others in the story only to surprise them later! But usually, dead means dead, and obviously so.

We have defined death in terms of separation, that moment when your soul (or spirit, if you prefer; see the last chapter for a discussion on this) departs from your physical body. But your body doesn't disappear instantly or even quickly. Why is this? Some would say that God mercifully leaves the body around to help mourners cope with their loss. But for some people this can add to their distress, as there is something unnatural about seeing a lifeless body, especially of someone you have known well. However, it may be far more distressing and harder to come to terms with the loss when there is no body to bury. Closure is more difficult to achieve.

Another reason why our body remains on earth is so that it can go back into the ground from which God created the physical part of our being. Ashes to ashes, dust to dust, as the saying goes. Our body belongs to this world, so it stays here, taking time to decompose (unless we burn it first) and once more become part of the earth from which God originally created humankind.

So far we have focused on the biological aspects of death. At this level we conclude that we die because our body is a biological machine which gradually wears out or suddenly stops functioning for some reason. But we haven't yet got to the heart of why this *must* happen at all. Is there an ultimate reason behind this? To answer this we must move from the biological realm to the theological.

The deeper reason for the certainty of death is because of sin. We are all sinful creatures, which is why we all die. To understand this we must once again go back to Genesis, and consider what has become known as the Fall. This is not a biblical term as such, but it does express well enough what happened to Adam and Eve, that is provided we don't think of the Fall as just a stumble or minor trip up from which we can easily pick ourselves up and carry on. The essence of this theological concept is that we are now fallen creatures in a fallen world. In fact, slightly better is to say that we are not so much fall*en* as fall*ing*. It is a continuous state rather than just a one-off historical event. We are now in freefall, unless God rescues us and starts to reverse this, a process we call redemption or salvation.

As we said before about the early part of Genesis, it does not matter so much whether you consider the account of the Fall in Genesis chapter 3 to be historically accurate in all details or that it is a story conveying certain truths. What does matter is that you accept that what is revealed there is indeed truth. The presence of symbolic elements in the text in no way contradicts the reality of its central meaning. Moreover, scripture elsewhere testifies to it being an actual event in some way (see 2 Cor. 11:3; Rom. 5:12; 1 Tim. 2:14), so we cannot just call it a myth, fable or legend, and leave it there. The impact of what happened at this point in human history is too serious for that, especially as the implication of our fallen nature is that we all die.

The account of the Fall illustrates the consequences of disobedience, and that one of these is death. Adam and Eve demonstrated a wilful disregard of what God wanted, coupled with a desire to be able to decide for themselves what is right and wrong regardless of what God had already decreed. We still see this all around us today in the way people live their lives. Living separately from God is a form of death even while we are alive. We refer to this as spiritual death, an expression we get from Ephesians 2:1 which refers to us being dead in our trespasses and sins. Ultimately, the price of our desire for independence from God is that we cut ourselves off from him permanently. Our final fate for rejecting God and his ways is eternal separation from him (more on this in a later chapter on hell).

God had warned Adam and Eve that if they ate from the tree of the knowledge of good and evil they would certainly die (Gen. 2:17). So when they did eat from that tree, judgement had to follow. This included physical death, but not immediately. They did not die on the spot. In fact, in Adam's case death did not come for centuries. According to Genesis 5:5, 'Adam lived a total of 930 years, and then he died.' Another part of God's judgement upon the first humans was to banish them from Eden so that they could not eat from another tree, the tree of life, otherwise they would have lived forever, immortal but immortalised as sinners.

The account of the Fall of Man provides the basis for the New Testament teaching on death and why it will be the experience of every one of us. For instance, in Romans Paul writes in very clear terms: 'Sin entered the world through one man, and death through sin, and in this way death came to all people, because all sinned' (Rom. 5:12). He adds in verse 17 that 'by the trespass of the one man, death reigned through that one man'.

In another letter, Paul upholds the same view that originally death came into the world though just one man by declaring, 'In Adam all die' (1 Cor. 15:22). And in Romans 6:23 we have one of Paul's most famous statements when he says, 'For the wages of sin is death', though perhaps we should talk about the just deserts of sin, as wages are usually something we look forward to receiving.

In all these verses, we can see that the two forms of death, spiritual and physical, are part of our world because of man's sinfulness, both in terms of the original sin of Adam and Eve and our continuing sinful lives. There is a profound connection between sin and death. Here is a reality that overshadows our lives, a reality that we cannot reverse. As sure as we are sinners, we are going to die.

But death as we experience it now was not part of God's original plan for his creation. In some sense, death is 'unnatural'. It is alien to this world, a by-product of man's sinfulness. Death is therefore to be regarded as a judgement upon us all, individually and collectively. It is a death *sentence*, even an execution.

Death is the outcome of living in a fallen world, a world in which our body cannot last forever. It has to die and rot and return to the ground. Death is thus an enemy, not a friend that releases us from our body as certain Greek ideas would have us believe (more in a later chapter). But it is our last enemy and one day death itself will be destroyed (see 1 Cor. 15:26; Rev. 20:14). Until then it remains a reality for us all.

In this chapter we have seen why death is inevitable from both a biological and a theological point of view. But what happens to us the moment after death? The answer is that we enter into what is usually referred to as the intermediate stage of our existence. This is the subject of our next chapter.

Chapter Six

The Intermediate State: Soul Sleep or the Time of Your Afterlife?

Last time we thought about why we die and considered both the biological and the theological reasons for death. But what happens next, after we have left our body behind on earth? In this chapter, and those that follow, we will focus on what is often called the intermediate state, that period between death and resurrection during which we are disembodied. If, as we have been saying, we do in some way survive the death of the body, then what kind of life follows? Is it a conscious existence involving activity, or a period of relative non-existence which often goes under the title of soul sleep?

The idea of soul sleep is rather misleading, and something the Bible does not teach at all. Soul sleep seems to suggest a sort of spiritual coma or, at best, a dreamlike quality of existence in which we are not involved in any kind of activity and not really conscious of anything going on around us. The next thing we will be aware of is the last trumpet announcing Christ's return (which will presumably be loud enough to wake us up!) followed by our own resurrection. Although for some this may seem like a reasonable understanding of the immediate afterlife, it has never found wide acceptance and few have taught it over church history. Indeed many, such as Calvin, wrote against it.

If soul sleep is biblically incorrect then where did the idea come from? After all, there are several places in scripture which seem to talk of death in terms of sleep, so what should we make of these?

For instance, on one occasion Jesus raised to life the daughter of a synagogue leader, telling the crowd inside the house that 'the girl is not dead but asleep' (Matt. 9:24). Clearly she *had* died, as testified by her father when he earlier implored Jesus to help him (Matt. 9:18). Similarly, in John 11:11-14, Jesus referred to Lazarus' death as being asleep and that he was going to wake him. The disciples thought he meant natural sleep so Jesus spelt it out to them, 'Lazarus is dead.' Later verses in the chapter also testify to him actually being dead (John 11:21, 44).

In Acts, the death of Stephen is described using the words 'he fell asleep' (Acts 7:60), and in his letters Paul often refers to believers who have 'fallen asleep' in contrast to those who are still living (see 1 Cor. 11:30, 15:6, 18, 20, 51; 1 Thess. 4:13-15, 5:10). Moreover, when preaching in Pisidian Antioch, Paul refers to David's death as 'he fell asleep' (Acts 13:36). Here he is picking up on an Old Testament phrase where 'slept with their fathers' (or ancestors) was simply an idiom for death and says nothing about any post-death experience.

Overall, sleep is used in the Bible as a euphemism or metaphorical expression for death. There are two reasons for this. One is to stress that for the believer death, just like sleep, is only temporary, and there is more to come when we 'wake up', also used metaphorically. The other reason is based on the body's outward appearance. From the perspective of those on earth it appears that once people die they are asleep. We cannot see any bodily activity, so we assume the soul is likewise inactive, but this is refuted in other parts of scripture which show conscious existence and even fellowship with God.

For instance, in Luke 20:37-38 Jesus affirms that the patriarchs, Abraham, Isaac and Jacob, are all alive to God. And towards the end of the same gospel, Jesus tells the thief on the cross that 'today you shall be with me in paradise' (Luke 23:43). We may wonder what Jesus meant by paradise (something we mention again in a later chapter) but the key point here is that on death the thief would be with Jesus and that this would happen immediately (today). There is no indication of any intervening period of soul sleep.

Also in Luke's gospel (16:19-31) there is the well-known parable of the rich man and Lazarus (not the same guy as in John chapter 11!). We will examine this story again in a later chapter but for now we see that Jesus is relating a situation within a post-death scenario (verse 22 tells us that both men had died). The references to body parts, such as 'finger' and 'tongue' in verse 24, suggest there are figurative elements to the story (as both men would be disembodied at this point), but this should not obscure the fact that neither were in a phase of soul sleep but rather were in a state of conscious existence. In fact, the use of the language of physicality in this story is a clear indication that the participants were alive in a way that must include being conscious.

Turning to Paul we find two significant passages. In Philippians 1:21-24, Paul is looking forward to a post-mortem existence out of his current body. For him, 'to die is gain' (v21), and his 'desire to depart and be with Christ' (v23) suggests he is anticipating a period of conscious blessedness in Christ's presence which will be 'better by far' than his present condition, though he recognises that staying in this world will be of greater benefit to God's people in Philippi.

Paul expresses similar wishes in 2 Corinthians 5:6-9, where he says he would prefer to be 'away from the body and at home with the Lord' (v8). Again Paul is envisaging a temporary disembodied state of existence. He describes our present life as being 'at home in the body' but 'away from the Lord' (v6), meaning that we are not currently in the direct immediate presence of Christ. But once 'the earthly tent we live in is destroyed' (v1) then we are at home with the Lord and can experience a heightened form of communion with him which surpasses anything known in this life. However, Paul adds that what he is looking forward to most of all is being re-clothed in a final new body (v2), something we will study more in a later chapter. So though Paul's view of the intermediate stage of the afterlife is superior to what we have now, it is not the most desirable part of what is to come after death. The blessing of Christ's direct presence may outweigh the downside of being disembodied, but a resurrected body is even better. The best is yet to come.

Moving away from Paul we find in Hebrews chapter 12 a heavenly scene of innumerable angels in joyful assembly together with the 'spirits of the righteous made perfect' (v23), which suggests that believers in Christ are at that point without a body but are already in a state of sinless perfection, even while awaiting the resurrection of the body to come.

Finally, in the book of Revelation we have two heavenly scenes in which the souls (or spirits) of those who have died are in the presence of God (Rev. 6:9-11, 7:9-10). They are praying, worshipping and crying out with a loud voice. They are definitely not sleeping. What is curious is that they have been given white robes and hold palm branches in their hands, so do they already have a new body? Rather, it is more likely that certain features here are more figurative than literal, as we saw earlier in Jesus' parable about the rich man and Lazarus. For instance, white robes represent righteousness. The idea that we receive our permanent resurrection bodies at death is difficult to sustain biblically. Indeed 2 Timothy 2:18 warns us against those who say the resurrection has already taken place. It is also worth adding that some who have had near-death experiences often claim to have seen a heaven that is populated with people already in bodies and with clothes, but it must be stressed that visions like this are personal rather than doctrinal, and should not override the biblical evidence.

Overall, the New Testament may not give us a single complete picture of what the intermediate state is like, but it is clear this is not soul sleep or a long period of unconsciousness. The post-mortem existence of the believer is something to look forward to, though not the ultimate bliss that awaits us.

One further question merits our attention at this point. If instead of soul sleep we have a conscious post-mortem existence, then will we still be aware of time passing? Indeed does the word 'time' have any meaning once we are no longer in this world? Here is another fascinating but complex question with a sense of mystery about it.

One thing we can assert is that God created time 'in the beginning' as an essential part of the structure of the cosmos. As such it was declared to be 'good' and there is nothing about the Fall of Man to suggest that this is no longer the case. Time will not cease to exist one day because it belongs to a fallen world. The Bible may talk of the 'end of the age' or even 'the end of this present evil age' but there is nothing evil about time itself. Moreover, after the 'end of the age' the Bible declares there is 'the age to come'. The correct biblical perspective is that one age leads into another.

What does time mean for us now? Someone has commented that time is what prevents everything happening all at once! That makes it extremely useful! But the serious point here is that currently we experience life sequentially, or, if you prefer, life is just one thing after another! Certainly this is the nature of time as we know it now. It is what makes life flow ever onwards.

For us, time is both a subjective experience and an objective fact. Time can seem rather fluid relative to what we are enjoying or enduring. We say things like 'time flies' or 'time is dragging'. But there is also ticking in the background a standardised version of time, known as 'clock time'. We need this in order to agree when something will happen, so that we arrive at events at 'the right time' rather than just 'when we feel like it'.

Time is a servant of God, created by him to serve his purposes, one of which was to provide order to this world. But he can modify it if he so chooses. He owns time rather than is constrained by it, as we are. Moreover, God can come into our time while remaining timeless himself. Only he can do this. We can never become timeless as he is. We can remember the past and anticipate the future, but we can only live in the present. It is part of our environment while on earth.

So what about the intermediate state? The view of soul sleep as mentioned earlier suggests we will not be aware of time. It may be ticking along on earth but we are effectively outside of time. Our next conscious moment will be our resurrection when time, in some sense, will be restored to us. Yet as we have seen, the idea of soul sleep is not biblical and should be discarded.

Being separated from our body and from this world may mean we will experience time rather differently from our current life. It may have a quality unlike anything we earth-dwellers can imagine now. But time will still exist. To eliminate all sense of temporal succession in the afterlife raises even bigger questions and flies in the face of what certain scriptures suggest.

For instance, in the book of Revelation there are scenes of heavenly worship involving falling down at the throne and the laying down of crowns. Such actions require a succession of time, as does singing and music which has to have a tempo or time element (Rev. 4:10, 5:9-12). Then in Revelation 6:10-11 the martyrs cry out using the phrase 'How long?' which is time based, as is the response when they are told to 'wait a little longer'. Neither question nor answer makes sense if there is no awareness of time passing. Later, in Revelation 7:15, we find the phrase 'serve him day and night in his temple', and the next chapter opens with the famous remark 'there was silence in heaven for half an hour' (Rev. 8:1). Even allowing for symbolism in such visions, it is difficult to dismiss entirely that time plays a role in the afterlife. Moreover, at the very end of Revelation we are told that in the new heaven and the new earth the tree of life yields its fruit 'every month' (Rev. 22:2). This corresponds with Isaiah's similar prophecy of the new heavens and the new earth where there will be new moons and Sabbaths (Isa. 66:22-23), a further indication of a time schedule, in this case based upon the longer timescale of a calendar.

Some may want to object to the above by pointing to the King James Version of Revelation 10:6 which reads 'there should be time no longer'. But this is a misleading translation, corrected in later versions, including the New King James Version and the New International Version. Here we have, 'There will be no more delay!' meaning there is little time left before God fulfils what he has set out to accomplish. Time is now short rather than about to cease completely. Time is not about to be extinguished as though it has done its job.

The phrase 'time will be no more' is not biblical. Unfortunately, errors like this are often spread through hymns and songs.

For instance, the hymn 'When the Roll is Called Up Yonder' opens with the line 'When the trumpet of the Lord shall sound and time shall be no more'. This gives a totally wrong impression. The song 'Amazing Grace' perhaps has a better grasp of the matter with 'When we've been there ten thousand years . . . we've no less days to sing God's praise . . .' which, allowing for poetic licence, does at least give some indication that time exists.

So we should conclude that time will exist in the afterlife. To be in any way conscious requires some kind of time progression. But the passing of time will not be a threat or a worry in the way it can be in this life, where we are often subject to time pressures. Time can create a hurried existence. We talk of time running out! Who hasn't had the nightmare that we can't get somewhere in time, or meet a deadline? For us now the passing of time also acts as a constant reminder that death is approaching. But in the afterlife we will no longer have such worries. Our future will be unlimited. We won't have to 'number our days'. We will be able to constantly delight in time. There will be no sense of boredom or striving to get something done in time. Perhaps there will remain a sense of past, present and future, but in such a way that the past is never really gone and the future is somehow radiating into the present.

To sum up, the intermediate state will be wonderful for Christians who will enjoy a more direct communion with Christ and a greater sense of God's presence than anything known in this life. We will be having the time of our afterlife! But however amazing it will be, this does not last forever. It is called 'intermediate' for a reason. There is more to come. Our final destiny is to be re-embodied ready for a new physical heaven and earth. Yet this is rarely taught and often ignored completely. We talk about dying and 'going to heaven' as though that's it, for ever and ever. At funerals the focus is on the deceased now being in a better place, at eternal rest, free from suffering. All this is true for a believer in Christ. But when it comes to talking about the new physicality ultimately awaiting them, there seems to be a reluctance, even a resistance. Why is this? We will pick this up in our next chapter.

Chapter Seven

Beware Greeks Bearing Ideas

We ended the last chapter by asking why many Christians regard the disembodied state to be their final destiny, rather than that of being re-embodied in a new physical universe. In this chapter we show that the answer lies in how the ideas of Greek philosophy entered the church early in its history and diverted it away from biblical truth. Overall, this is a large story with implications in many areas of Christianity and we will meet this again later. Meanwhile, here is a brief survey to introduce these ideas and show their impact on a Christian view of the afterlife.

Much of the misunderstanding about the afterlife comes from Greek thinking, so we should start by clarifying what we mean by this and who was involved. We use the phrase 'Greek thinking' to specifically refer to the later period of Greek history and, in particular, to the philosophy of Plato (428–348 BC). Plato had been a pupil of Socrates (c. 470–399 BC) and he later went on to teach Aristotle (384–322 BC). Aristotle in turn became the tutor of Alexander the Great (356–323 BC), a military leader who conquered the then known world and with this success he spread the worldview based upon the teaching of Plato, which became known as Hellenism. This expansion of Greek culture and philosophy continued into the Roman Empire which followed, and from there into Western civilisation as we know it.

The main idea behind Plato's philosophy is usually referred to as dualism, a term which signifies the division of reality into two distinct parts: the spiritual and the physical (or material). These are opposites and in conflict with each other. The spiritual world represents the realm of goodness, truth and beauty, whereas the physical world is fallen and evil. In short, spiritual good, material bad, which leads to all kinds of consequences and implications. One in particular is that our physical body is bad, while our inner soul (or spirit) is good.

In dualism, the soul is the real 'me'. The body is regarded as inferior, merely the vessel I inhabit during my earthly life. In fact, our body is actually a hindrance to true life, a liability not an asset. It opposes, even imprisons, our soul which longs to be set free from its physical surrounding. Plato even went so far as to refer to our body as the tomb of the soul. His famous pronouncement on this can be summed up as '*soma sema*', literally 'flesh tomb'.

All this is in direct contradiction to the biblical view of man. In an earlier chapter we saw how in Genesis 2:7 God breathed the breath of life into the dust of Adam's body and created an integrated living being. God did not entrap a soul in an existing physical body, nor did he create body and soul as antagonists. Rather, they were perfectly fitted for each other in a way that defines our total human nature. In that sense, my body is just as much 'me' as is my soul.

Also, it is wrong to suggest that evil entered the world because of Adam and Eve's fleshly physicality. It was not because they had a body that the first humans fell away from God. Indeed, it could be argued that their desire for rebellion and the decision to disobey came from within their innermost being, from their soul. Certainly their will and mind were involved. Obviously, so was the body and is now also part of our fallen nature, but it was originally an inherently good and essential aspect of our human nature and so is capable of being redeemed and perfected as part of a glorious new humanity.

Another consequence of dualism is that God, who is pure spirit, must remain distant from the material world. If all matter is evil, then God cannot be directly involved in the physical world in any way. The two must be kept apart. We can't have God 'getting his hands dirty'! This must also apply to the moment of creation itself, so according to Platonic thinking, when it came to creating his world God had to use agents to do it for him, intermediaries known as demiurges.

Another aspect of Platonic philosophy concerns the pre-existence of souls in the spiritual realm before they come into this world. Plato taught that the souls of every person destined to live on earth were created at the same time and then 'stored' in a spiritual or heavenly realm while awaiting the point at which God brings the soul to earth to be joined with the body as it grows in the womb. So before entering its physical 'prison' the soul had enjoyed all the benefits of dwelling in the spiritual realm, communing with the essences of goodness, beauty, truth, and all the other abstract 'spiritual' qualities we are now aware of. As a result, each of us is born with some pre-existing knowledge of these things which we then ‘re-learn’ in the context of this life by simply recalling what the soul already knows from its former existence. This idea of ‘learning through recollection’ is very different from the more common view that we enter this world as blank slates ready to learn all things from birth. Called *tabula rasa* (meaning ‘clean slate’), this says we do not have a head start in terms of innate knowledge, though we do come into this world with longings for truth, beauty and goodness which we have gained directly from our maker within our God-breathed *nefesh*.

The possibility that our soul might have had an earlier existence in heaven has no support in scripture. Rather, we simply did not exist beforehand. So is there a Christian view of the origin of the soul? There are two main ideas, known as creationism and traducianism.

Creationism argues that God creates a new soul for each person and places it within that person’s body, either at conception or sometime between conception and birth. Traducianism, on the other hand, says that the soul as well as the body is inherited from both parents at the time of conception. Luther favoured this latter view, while Calvin preferred creationism, which is now held by most evangelicals. It also has more biblical support. Under creationism a new child is seen as a gift from God, a co-operation between God and humanity, rather than being entirely a product of human procreation.

From what we have already said about dualism it is not surprising that, for Plato, death was not something to be feared but welcomed. Here was the moment when the immortal soul was released from its prison and could return to the spiritual life of bliss that it longed for. Socrates had also previously argued that death was not a bad thing, claiming that the soul's aim was to escape the body and never return to anything similar. This was taken up by Plato, whose worldview involved the aspiration of the soul to transcend this present world of matter and attain a higher reality. To achieve this, the soul had to be purified during this life through the pursuit of wisdom and truth. Failure meant the soul would undergo an endless cycle of death and rebirth in a physical form. This was known as the transmigration of souls, which seems very similar to the idea of reincarnation.

Once again, we see that this philosophically based Greek thinking is contrary to the Hebraic thinking found within the Bible. Certainly the Bible says we need to be delivered from our current bodies, which are subject to sin and decay. However, the promise of God to us is not a future without a body but rather the attainment of a new body. God made us both physical and spiritual so a spirit without a body is incomplete and incompatible with how we are meant to be. Such a state is so alien to us that we struggle to imagine what this might be like and our attempts to describe it remain limited. Moreover, it can be said that without the redemption of the body then it is difficult to claim that humankind has been redeemed in the fullest sense.

All we have been discussing so far is not just of historical interest. It addresses directly our earlier question about why Christians today talk of dying and going to heaven rather than being re-embodied in a new physical universe. It also impacts other areas of the Christian faith. Plato was not only innovative in the philosophical arena, he was also highly influential in many ways. Dualism became more and more widespread, and Platonic ideas soon made inroads into the early church and Christian thinking generally. How did this happen?

To find an answer we need to go to the city of Alexandria on the north coast of Egypt. Named after Alexander the Great who founded it in 331 BC as part of his military conquest and desire to spread Greek culture and philosophy, it quickly grew to be one of the greatest cities of the Hellenistic world, second only to Rome in size and wealth. It also became home to a new school of theological thought which promoted the latest Greek ideas and brought them into the Christian faith.

Before we see how Hellenism influenced Christianity, we ought to mention a certain Jew named Philo who lived in Alexandria early in the first century (c. 20 BC to AD 50). He so admired Greek culture and Plato's philosophy that he wanted to incorporate these into Judaism. He especially argued that the Jewish scriptures should be interpreted allegorically rather than literally. In an allegory the true meaning of a text is not found through a plain or obvious reading of the words used, or a literal understanding of any objects mentioned. These simply provide clues to help us uncover the deeper spiritual message which is contained beneath the surface of the text. This emphasis on the underlying spiritual meaning of a text clearly appealed to the Greek mindset and so became the natural way to interpret scripture and discover its truth.

Not long after Philo, Greek thinking began to infiltrate the Christian church and by the second and third centuries it was well established. Particularly responsible for this were two men who lived and worked in Alexandria. One was Clement (AD 150–215), the other was Origen (AD 185–254). Clement of Alexandria, as he was known, became the head of the theological school there and, following Philo, he too applied the allegorical method to biblical texts, including now the New Testament. His successor as leader of the school at Alexandria was Origen, who systematised this technique further. For him, the spiritual or allegorical method of interpretation was the highest form of seeking biblical truth. Such was his influence that many today still feel this is the correct approach, especially regarding prophetic passages or even the Old Testament generally.

Some may argue that Clement, Origen and others were simply taking up what they saw as the output of the best minds of their times, but mixing this with the Christian faith was a dangerous error that was bound to produce negative consequences for Christianity. Allowing Greek thinking to infiltrate the message of the Old Testament and of Jesus and the apostles could never produce anything good. It was like adding poison into the bloodstream. Trying to update or improve Christianity using Platonic thinking was at best dubious, at worst a treacherous move with far-reaching repercussions.

What began in the second and third centuries continued into the fourth. A new version of Platonic philosophy emerged called Neoplatonism (new Platonism) which continued to fuse the ideas of Plato with Christian teaching. For the Neoplatonists the Divine One of their philosophy was the same as the heavenly Father of the Bible. Plato's dualism had divided reality into a higher world of perfect ideals, or Forms, and a lower world of earthly phenomena. If we contemplate these eternal Forms (such as beauty, truth and justice), and reject the everyday material things of our earthly lives, then we can ultimately ascend to this Supreme Being and leave this physical world behind completely and forever.

One of the dominant thinkers of this era was Augustine of Hippo (AD 354–430). He rejected the physical reign of Christ on earth, known as the Millennium, and instead systematised the idea of Amillennialism in which, on death, we go straight to a spiritual heaven and stay there rather than return to earth with Christ. Moreover, our next life will not contain any physical objects, such as trees and rivers, such as are found in Revelation chapters 21 and 22. God may have talked in these terms to help us gain a better understanding, but we must see beyond them to something purely spiritual. Likewise, Augustine's vision of the City of God was not the new Jerusalem, coming down from heaven as a dwelling place for God among men. Rather it was a spiritual city, an eternal spirit home in which we only think about God and worship him. There is nothing else to do or enjoy. All connection with anything earthly has come to an end.

Such thinking was the norm in mainstream Christianity for centuries, but more was to come in the twelfth and thirteenth centuries with the birth of a new theological movement called Scholasticism. Here the leading figure was Thomas Aquinas (1225–1274). He followed the ideas of Aristotle, a pupil of Plato, so the scholastic view of a future heavenly existence was also entirely intangible. Nothing physical was allowed. So in the centuries that followed the rise of Scholasticism with its underlying Platonic views, Greek thinking continued to prevail. Although the Reformation started to reverse this to some extent, Hellenism has never entirely lost its grip on the Western church.

The main point in all this is that whenever Platonists of any kind became part of the Christian church, their background in Greek thinking proved too difficult for them to renounce. They never allowed their minds to be transformed by the Word of God. Instead, Plato remained the lens through which they interpreted the Bible, the Christian message, and even Jesus himself. But Platonic thinking is diametrically opposed to Christianity in many ways. In particular, by promoting the freeing of the spirit never to return to anything remotely like a body, it destroys any hope of physical resurrection. For Plato, the body and the soul are temporarily bound together in an imperfect first world from which the soul must escape into a perfect second world. Life on earth is merely a prelude to this.

From very early in its history much of the church was seduced by Platonism and never fully recovered, so nowadays people assume these ideas must be in the Bible somewhere and be part of the Christian faith. But Platonic teaching is an insult to Christ's incarnation, redemption and resurrection. He did not die to give disembodied people an eternity in a spirit realm. He died to restore to us the fullness of our humanity as part of the redemption of creation generally.

A great loss was incurred when the original Hebraic nature of God's Word and of Christianity was devalued by Hellenism. Effectively, the Bible was treated as a playground for philosophers to explore their own ideas and theories rather than to discover God's truth. To reverse this loss requires a recovery of a Hebraic understanding of the Bible and of the Christian faith.

In this chapter we have attempted a brief overview of how Greek thinking infiltrated the church. We can now see why Christians today largely talk of a disembodied future rather than a new body in a new physical universe. It will also help us with some of the topics to come in later chapters. Meanwhile, in our next chapter we will consider an important concept of the afterlife found in the Old Testament, namely Sheol.

Chapter Eight

Sheol

We are currently investigating what is known as the intermediate state, that period between death and resurrection during which we are disembodied. In this chapter we will investigate what the Old Testament has to say on this and, in particular, its use of the Hebrew word *sheol*.

We may wonder if the Old Testament can really contribute anything useful to our study of the afterlife. After all, we now have the later revelation of the New Testament and the resurrection of Jesus. Is there any point in examining *sheol* other than out of historical interest? But, as always, the Old Testament contributes towards the progressive revelation of scripture as a whole, and it is worth knowing how the ancient Israelites viewed what came after death. The writers of the Old Testament may not have had as much insight as their New Testament counterparts but they did ask the same questions about survival after death. Moreover, from their own scriptures they did have a more advanced idea of an afterlife than other cultures of the time, such as that of Egypt.

Sheol is the most commonly used word in the Old Testament to depict post-mortem existence and the realm of the dead. It occurs about 65 times in all and features throughout every period of biblical Hebrew. Its etymological origin is disputed but most favour a root meaning of 'desolate world' or 'the un-world'. *Sheol* can be translated in various ways. Sometimes it is simply 'pit', but more usually it is 'hell' or 'grave', in roughly equal numbers. However, both of these can be misleading. This is not the same idea of hell that we meet later in the Bible, the place of eternal punishment for the wicked. Nor does it equate to our usual understanding of grave as a tomb or burial place, usually just a few feet under the ground.

Although in some contexts *sheol* can mean grave as in a burial plot, it implies much more. In fact, there is another Hebrew word, *kever*, which means grave and only that, so there is an alternative to *sheol* if grave is all that is meant. *Sheol* is more than just where the body rests. It is the place where the spirits of the dead are gathered. We shall see the importance of understanding 'the grave' as the place of the dead, rather than just a tomb, later in this book. Moreover, *sheol* also implies depth. Unlike a grave for the body, *sheol* was regarded as being a long way down, in the uttermost depths of the earth.

The Old Testament writers believed the soul survived the death of the body and departed to an underground world. This happened to everyone, righteous or wicked. But to be in *sheol* after death was a gloomy experience, an undesirable shadowy existence. In fact, the spirits there are described as 'shades' (*rephaim*), shadows of their former selves. Proverbs 9:18 captures this well: 'the dead are there' uses the word *rephaim*, and 'deep in the realm of the dead' translates 'the depths of *sheol*'.

Overall, *sheol* has two meanings. One is synonymous with death itself, or the state of being dead. The other is a place for departed spirits, disembodied but conscious. So while the Old Testament suggests some kind of life immediately after death, it only provides a rather underdeveloped picture of a shadowy or diminished existence in what could be thought of as the underworld.

We will look now at specific texts that use the word *sheol,* starting with the seven occurrences in the Pentateuch.

The first of these is in Genesis 37:35 where Jacob, on the presumed death of Joseph, says he will go down to *sheol* in mourning for his son. This is one case where translators often use the word grave for *sheol,* as though Jacob is saying he will mourn for Joseph until the day of his own death when he will join his son in the grave. However, what Jacob is most likely expressing here is not that one day he will be buried alongside Joseph, but that the loss of his son is making him feel now just as desolate as though he was dead himself. He is so grief-stricken that it seems like the complete end of everything. Life is effectively over for him.

The other three texts in Genesis also reflect Jacob's grief, this time expressed as 'bringing down his grey hairs with sorrow to *sheol*' (see Gen. 42:38, 44:29, 31). Of the rest of the Pentateuch, Deuteronomy 32:22 simply translates *sheol* as the realm of the dead below, which is also the case in the book of Numbers, but here slightly more is involved. In Numbers 16:28-34 we read the account of the rebellion of Korah and his followers. Their punishment was to be swallowed up by the earth with all they possessed, dramatically described in verses 31 and 33 as being 'taken alive down to *sheol*'. The immediate impact of this was so great that the whole of Israel feared this might be about to happen to them too! This event clearly had a lasting effect upon the nation and perhaps developed their understanding of *sheol* as an underground world for the dead. We also find a later echo of this in Psalm 55:15, where David writes, 'Let death take my enemies by surprise; let them go down alive to the realm of the dead.' Clearly the phrase 'taken alive down to *sheol*' isn't suggesting they continued to live there physically. They *were* killed when the earth opened up! But visually it would appear as though they were being taken alive, as their bodies disappeared from sight. There was nothing left to bury.

The psalmists, like Jacob above, also frequently used the word *sheol* to describe their personal anguish and feelings of dread even while still alive in this world. Psalm 88 is particularly graphic, 'I am counted among those who go down to the pit' (v4). 'I am set apart with the dead, like the slain who lie in the grave' (v5), another instance where grave means the realm of the departed not a burial plot. Regarding those in *sheol* the same verse goes on to describe them as those 'whom you remember no more, who are cut off from your care'. Then in verse 10 the psalmist cries out, 'Do you show your wonders to the dead? Do their spirits rise up and praise you?'

This gloomy portrayal of *sheol* is repeated elsewhere in the psalms. For instance, in Psalm 30:9 David says, 'What is gained if I am silenced, if I go down to the pit? Will the dust praise you? Will it proclaim your faithfulness?' Overall, the psalms refer to *sheol* as a place of abandonment (Ps. 16:10), and of shame and silence (Ps. 31:17).

Hezekiah expressed similar sentiments on his recovery from the serious illness that had brought him close to death. He praised God for his love that had kept him from 'the pit of destruction', adding that 'the grave cannot praise you [and] those who go down to the pit cannot hope for [God's] faithfulness' (Isa. 38:17-18). Another bleak view of *sheol*.

As we might expect, Ecclesiastes also portrays a rather negative view of the afterlife. He tells us that at least the living know they will die but the dead know nothing at all; they have no further reward and even their name is forgotten (Eccl. 9:5). He adds in verse 10, that in the realm of the dead, where you are going, there is neither working nor planning nor knowledge nor wisdom, though he does seem to have a positive motive in saying this, namely to affirm life now. Live each day to the full and work hard while you are alive.

We should perhaps contrast what Ecclesiastes says with what we read in Isaiah chapter 14. Here is a vivid picture of the inhabitants of *sheol* receiving the king of Babylon into their midst. The realm of the dead below is all astir to meet him at his coming; the spirits of the departed are aroused to greet him. But they welcome him with taunts. The oppressor has come to his end. Those who were once kings over the nations also 'become weak, as we are; you have become like us'. Powerful people all end up in the same place; all are equally brought down to the realm of the dead, to the depths of the pit (see especially vv4, 9-10, 15). So in this chapter we learn a bit more about *sheol*. There is conscious activity there and it is not an impersonal place where you can hide from your past. Those who are there remain known for who they are and what they've done. So perhaps, contrary to what Ecclesiastes thought, in *sheol* our name is not forgotten after all, and certain kinds of knowledge do exist there.

Overall, the concept of *sheol* reveals much about belief in the afterlife during the Old Testament period. For a start, it shows a conviction that the soul did indeed survive death. Moreover, all souls went to *sheol*. No-one could avoid this. *Sheol* was a great leveller, the norm for everyone. As for where it was, *sheol* was thought to be in the lowest parts of the earth, though whether its location can really be described in physical terms at all is rather doubtful. It was more a nebulous un-place where souls existed as *rephaim* or 'shades' of their former selves. However, it seems they were self-aware and conscious of their surroundings though details about the degree of consciousness and activity are somewhat vague.

Another feature of *sheol* is that it seems to be a place of no return. You were locked away with no hope of escape, forgotten forever. Yet there are occasional glimpses in the Old Testament this might not be the case. For instance, in Psalm 49:15 the psalmist declares that 'God will redeem me from the realm of the dead; he will surely take me to himself', though it is not clear what he thought this redemption might be like.

Then there is the intriguing story in 1 Samuel chapter 28 when the spirit of Samuel was 'brought up' from the depths of *sheol* to talk to Saul, though he presumably returned there afterwards. We shall look at this event again in a later chapter but for now we can say that this is something that was usually forbidden, though Moses and Elijah experienced something similar at the transfiguration of Jesus.

Another question is whether *sheol* was the same for everyone there, righteous and wicked alike. Some have argued that actually only the wicked are there. Certainly Psalm 9:17 states that 'the wicked go down to the realm of the dead', but does this imply only the wicked? And where would the righteous go if not to *sheol*? No alternative is ever mentioned in the Old Testament so it is best to assume *sheol* was for all, however good or bad they had been. But if this is the case, did the wicked and the righteous have the same experiences in the afterlife? Or did they have separate destinies within *sheol*?

Some have suggested there might have been different regions in *sheol*, with a lower region for the most wicked. This is not expressly stated in the Old Testament, though it seems some rabbis did later teach that *sheol* had two distinct compartments. It must be stressed, however, that this division of *sheol* did not equate in any way to the eventual idea of heaven and hell that we find in the New Testament.

It also appears that some in the early church taught that the Old Testament saints existed in an upper level of *sheol* so that they could be delivered from there later by the risen Christ. But, again, there is no biblical evidence for this and it seems to be a rather retrospective idea based upon the later New Testament.

So perhaps it is now time to turn to the New Testament and, in particular, to what Jesus taught, so our next chapter will focus on *hades*, the Greek equivalent of *sheol*.

Chapter Nine

Hades

In our study of the intermediate state, the period between death and resurrection during which we are disembodied, we have looked at what the Old Testament has to say on this through the word *sheol*. We ended with certain questions hanging as to whether everyone, righteous and wicked alike, all experienced the same in *sheol* or whether there were two distinct compartments. Now we move on to the New Testament and the Greek equivalent, *hades*, to find out if this settles the matter and see what more we can learn on this particular aspect of the afterlife.

We should start by stressing that the gospel accounts are primarily set within Old Testament times. The new covenant didn't come into effect at the start of the gospel story with the birth of Jesus but at the end with his death and resurrection. We should be especially aware of this regarding the teaching of Jesus, as he is addressing those whose understanding still lies within the framework of the Judaism of the day even if he is bringing more light on these matters.

Also at this point we should emphasise that *hades* is not to be equated with hell. Hell is the final eternal destiny of the wicked after the last judgement, and should not be confused with the provisional nature of *hades* within the intermediate state. The two are quite distinct. Some older translations, such as the King James Version, may render *hades* as hell, but this is incorrect and is usually put right in later versions. *Hades* is not the translational equivalent of hell but of *sheol*, as seen from the Greek translation of the Old Testament, known as the Septuagint (LXX). As such, *hades* refers to the realm of the dead in the same way as does *sheol*. An example of this is in Acts 2:27, 'you will not abandon me to the realm of the dead'. Here Peter quotes Psalm 16:10, where *sheol* in the psalm becomes *hades* in Acts.

There are two views concerning the derivation of the word *hades*. Some think its origin reflects the idea of 'not seen' or 'out of sight', which would make sense, but more likely it comes from a word meaning 'all receiving', as after death everyone goes there without exception. As for its use in English, the word *hades* is a transliteration, meaning it is formed directly from the original Greek letters by turning them letter-by-letter into their English equivalents. For many the idea of *hades* is familiar from its designation of the underworld in Greek mythology, but we must beware of automatically transferring anything we know about this into our biblical thinking. Rather we should examine what the New Testament texts say on this matter, and this we will now do.

Perhaps surprisingly, the word *hades* is used rather sparingly in the New Testament. For instance, it occurs only four times in the gospels, and always within the teaching of Jesus. These are Matthew 11:23 (paralleled in Luke 10:15),

Matthew 16:18 and Luke 16:23. As for Acts, the word appears only twice, in 2:27 and 2:31, where Peter declares that the resurrection of Jesus means he was not left in *hades*, the realm of the dead, something we will explore more later. Finally, we find mention of *hades* a few more times within the book of Revelation, namely Revelation 1:18, 6:8 and 20:13-14. These verses offer some important details for us to look at later in this chapter. We should add that some versions seem to mention *hades* in 1 Corinthians 15:55 (quoting Hos. 13:14), but the best manuscripts do not have this particular Greek word. Rather there is a repeat of *thanate*, meaning death, and so a better translation is 'Where, O death, is your sting?', a parallel to the first part of the verse, 'Where, O death, is your victory?'

We will now look at some of these texts in detail, starting with those in the gospels. In Matthew 11:23 (also Luke 10:15) Jesus predicts that Capernaum, in punishment for its unbelief, will 'go down to Hades'. What does this mean? Can a city actually go to *hades*? Or is this figurative language for something? One suggestion is that it refers to the ultimate doom of its unbelieving inhabitants; it is they that will go down to *hades*. But we know they would anyway as everyone does! So, instead, others argue this is not about the fate of its people as such, but it is intended as a metaphor for the city's humiliation. *Hades*, like *sheol*, speaks of great depths, so here Jesus is predicting that Capernaum will be brought low. It will suffer the same fate as Sodom, judged and reduced to nothing historically. Support for this idea is found in the contrasting phrase 'lifted up to the heavens', also in verse 23, which means receiving acclamation and honour. Capernaum will enjoy none of this. Instead it will go down in history in shame for its failure to recognise the Messiah in its midst.

The second gospel reference is in Matthew 16:18. Here Jesus declares that the gates of *hades* shall not overcome the church, or rather the community, that he will build. It is often noted that at this point in time Jesus and his disciples are in the region of Caesarea Philippi, a significant site of pagan worship which featured a cave believed by the locals to be a gateway to the underworld (or *hades*). In particular, this was where the god Pan could travel between this world and the underworld. This would certainly give Jesus a useful visual aid to make his point, but, as we said before, we must not let ideas from Greek mythology define our thinking. Equally, as *hades* is not hell, we should also avoid assuming this verse is about the church being able to resist any demonic assault that may come upon them from *hades*. There is no evidence that demonic spirits dwelt in *hades* or visited this world from there. Nor is there mention of Satan in *hades* anywhere in the Bible. Instead we should base our understanding upon the fact that *hades* is the realm of the dead, and as such was deemed to be a stronghold of the power of death. This is where everyone ended up and from which no-one could escape. Hence the reference in this verse to the *gates* of *hades*, which were thought to be locked forever against us, creating a prison for our souls. It is here where Jesus' teaching hits home. Those who believe in him will *not* be held in *hades* forever. There *is* hope of escape for those who belong to his community. The message is the same as that in Acts 2:27, namely that God will not abandon his people and leave them in *hades* forever. God did not allow this to happen to Jesus, as his resurrection proves, so we can be confident of this for ourselves too. The gates of *hades* ultimately have no power over you. They will not keep you trapped there forever. You may go there when you die but this is not your final destiny. You will be redeemed from *hades*.

We now come to the gospel passage which provides the most detail about *hades* and the most difficulties. In Luke 16:19-31 we have the story of the rich man and Lazarus, where the word *hades* occurs in verse 23. What can we learn from this passage?

The first point is to recognise that this passage takes the form of a story, or parable. As such it contains figurative elements which, if taken literally, might undermine what we already know. For instance, we read of Lazarus' finger and the rich man's tongue (v24), but both men are now disembodied. They both died (v22) so they have no physical bodies. The body parts are therefore symbolic, as indeed may also be the reference to fire, also in verse 24. Then we have angels carrying Lazarus after death to Abraham's side (or bosom, in older translations). The role of the angels here can have meaning within the story without us assuming that this is automatically the case for every righteous person. Then there is Abraham himself, who is effectively the main character in the story and responsible for conveying the actual teaching that occurs here. It seems Jesus wanted to put his own words into the mouth of Abraham for greater effect within the story. However, we should be clear that none of these figurative elements detract from the truth being taught here, though we do need to appreciate their role within the story format.

It should also be noted that while the afterlife provides the main setting for this story, its initial subject matter concerns money, especially wrong attitudes towards personal wealth and the poor. It was probably told in the hearing of some money-loving Pharisees who were sneering at Jesus (Luke 16:14). It has been argued that Jesus is here not so much teaching about the afterlife as how to live better in this life. Some say we should focus on this rather than on what he says about *hades* which is merely the backdrop. While there is some validity to this, and we certainly should not ignore the money aspect of the story, it would be wrong to assume what Jesus says here about *hades* is not relevant or not accurate. Jesus would not invent or manipulate details about *hades* just to make his story more compelling, so we can trust this aspect of the story also.

However, as we said earlier, we also need to recognise that what we read in the gospel accounts is still largely set within the framework of Old Testament thinking and will reflect the Judaism of the day. So, of necessity, Jesus here is using terms, such as *hades* and 'Abraham's side', that will be familiar to his audience. But is this all he is doing, or is he actually endorsing these views as his own? Or maybe he simply starts where they are in order to add more teaching of his own?

Unlike the other references to *hades* in the gospels, this passage contains the idea of punishment. In verse 23, we see the rich man 'in Hades, where he was in torment'. In verse 24 he declares, 'I am in agony in this fire', and in verse 28 he describes where he is as a 'place of torment'. It is comments like these which lead us to associate *hades* with punishment and pain, though we should stress again this is not the same as hell, the final destiny of the wicked after the last judgement.

In our chapter on *sheol* we asked if everyone who went there had the same experience, righteous and wicked alike. From the Old Testament alone this wasn't clear, though some rabbis began to teach that *sheol* had two distinct compartments with very different outcomes. This story of Jesus may suggest he is upholding this.

Certainly the story of Lazarus and the rich man relates a stark disparity between their fates. In contrast to the suffering of the rich man, Lazarus is in a place where he is being comforted (v25). But there are two possible opinions on this: either Lazarus is in *hades* but a different part of it (known as Abraham's bosom or side) or he is in another place entirely. Overall, this remains a tricky issue to resolve.

Verse 23 is the only verse containing the word *hades* but it is a little ambiguous. It makes it clear this is where the rich man is but without necessarily excluding Lazarus being there also. Nor does any other verse, so to insist that he isn't there is to argue from silence. Moreover, the main emphasis in verse 23 is not on *hades* itself as a place but on the torment the rich man is experiencing there. So it may be that Lazarus is also in *hades* but in a non-suffering part, distinct from that of the rich man. But then in the previous verse (v22) Lazarus is carried by angels to Abraham's side. Perhaps this mention of angels indicates a different destination entirely from that of the rich man, maybe even that Lazarus was taken into God's presence?

It might help us to decide where Lazarus went if we knew where Abraham was. All we are told is that he was 'far away' from where the rich man was (v23). Again this seems rather inconclusive. Is it possible that Abraham could be in *hades*? Some in the early church taught that the Old Testament saints existed in an upper level of *sheol*, but there is no evidence for this in the Hebrew scriptures. It is likely this idea came from working backwards from this gospel story.

Also in this story we read that Lazarus and the rich man can see each other and communicate, but not cross over to each other due to a great chasm set in place to deter anyone from trying. So from all the evidence we have, we can understand why, on balance, for many this story offers convincing proof of two distinct regions within *hades* rather than a separate place elsewhere. This has been the standard teaching of most Christian denominations from early times, with just a few variations. The message being that after death we go to either a place of suffering or a place of comfort. The latter might even be enjoyable, but there is no neutral place in *hades*.

Two final thoughts before we leave this passage. Perhaps we should not be thinking in terms of places at all, but rather of states of being. Naturally we are drawn into thinking of geographical locations, or places, as we know them now, but this may be distorting what we read in this story. In a disembodied state, dimensional spaces may not be relevant. So perhaps the above debate is rather artificial and we should try reading the passage without analysing it too closely regarding which 'parts' or 'compartments' are involved.

Secondly, we need to recognise that the Bible takes us on a journey of progressive revelation and this passage in Luke 16 comes before Jesus' resurrection. At the end of the gospel Jesus says to the dying thief, 'You will be with me in paradise' (Luke 23:43). We don't ask where in *hades* this is. Rather, we focus on that fact that he will be with Jesus (not with Abraham!). Paul similarly talks about being 'at home with the Lord' after death (2 Cor. 5:8, cf Phil. 1:23). We can rejoice over this truth without needing to work out 'where' this is.

Having mentioned the progressive revelation of the Bible, it is fitting we end this chapter on *hades* by turning to the book of Revelation itself, where we find some good news.

Firstly, in Revelation 1:18 we learn that Jesus holds 'the keys of death and Hades'. In this verse death and *hades* are presented as prisons from which Christ has the power to deliver us by virtue of his own resurrection. 'I am the Living One; I was dead, and now look, I am alive for ever and ever!' (v18). So even over *hades* Jesus is now in full charge. This is similar to Matthew 16:18 where we saw that the gates of *hades* have no power to keep us locked in there. Now we see why. Jesus has the key and has opened the way for us.

In all the references to *hades* in Revelation the phrase 'death and *hades*' is a common feature. In Revelation 6:8, death is personified as riding a horse, in particular a pale horse. *Hades* is not far behind, which makes sense as it is the destination of those whom death will claim. This verse is the opening of the fourth seal and is the final fling of death before the world comes to the end of the present age. Death and *hades* themselves are soon to meet their own demise.

This demise is illustrated in Revelation 20:13-14. Here, death and *hades* deliver up all the dead that they are still holding in readiness for the final judgement. Once emptied of all the remaining dead, both are then thrown into the lake of fire. So we should remember in all we have discussed in this chapter that *hades* is only temporary. It has no eternal role in God's plan. After all, if there is to be no more death in the new heaven and the new earth (Rev. 21:4), then there can be no *hades* either. It has no further use. Its destruction is guaranteed.

We will return to some of these points in later chapters. Meanwhile, there are more aspects of the intermediate afterlife for us to study. Next we will consider the topic of purgatory.

Chapter Ten

Purgatory

As part of our current studies on what is known as the intermediate state, the period between death and resurrection during which we are disembodied, we will be focusing in this chapter on the idea of purgatory. Many will have heard of this but have little knowledge of what it entails. Here we will try and understand a topic which typically produces scepticism or confusion.

Purgatory is primarily a Catholic doctrine though a few Protestants have embraced it to some degree, most notably the Anglican writer C.S. Lewis (see, for instance, *A Grief Observed* and *Letters to Malcolm*, 'Letter 20'). But many Christians question the validity of the doctrine or believe it to be totally unfounded. Some Catholics even wonder if the Catholic Church dropped it some time ago, yet within Catholicism, purgatory is still seen as an essential part of the scheme of salvation.

We should start with a simple definition and overview of purgatory. Purgatory can be described as a place of suffering where the souls of believers are purified from sin until they are ready to be admitted into heaven. This might surprise some. Souls of *believers*? Until *ready* for heaven?

But this is the main point. Purgatory is not the same as hell, nor is it to be associated with the punishment of the damned. Those in purgatory are not on their way to hell as though this is some kind of foretaste. They are assured of salvation and on their way to heaven, but they still have to undergo purification through suffering in order 'to achieve the holiness necessary to enter the joy of heaven' (Paragraph 1030 of the Catechism of the Catholic Church).

So, to be clear, there are still only two final destinations: heaven and hell. Purgatory is part of the intermediate state; it is not a final state. No soul remains there forever or is being prepared for hell. On the contrary, a soul spends time there in preparation for a holy heaven. The sufferings in purgatory may be greater than anything in this life but are far less than those of hell from which there is no escape. So these sufferings are endurable as heaven is guaranteed afterwards. They can also be seen as positive and profitable as through them you are working off the remaining debt caused by certain sins committed while on earth. Such sufferings thus satisfy a just and holy God, being presented to him in atonement for various sins in compensation for the punishment believers should have received in their earthly life.

This clearly does not accord with the Protestant view of salvation by grace through faith in Christ's one-off atoning sacrifice on the cross for all our sins. For instance, 1 John 1:7 tells us that 'the blood of Jesus, his Son, purifies us from all sin' (see also Rom. 6:10; Col. 2:13-14; Heb. 9:28; 1 Pet. 3:18). So how did the idea of purgatory come about? Can it really be part of God's plan of salvation? For this, we need to examine other aspects of Catholicism, and place purgatory within the wider issues of sin, baptism, confession and penance.

Catholicism, like Protestantism, recognises that we are all born in sin and come under judgement. We deserve eternal punishment and can only be reconciled back to God through Christ's death and resurrection. Protestants believe this comes about through repentance and faith. Catholics believe that this judgement is removed through the sacrament of baptism, usually performed on babies or infants. At that point a person moves from a state of sin into a state of grace. Baptism is thus a strong sacrament. It removes both guilt and punishment but it is not repeatable. So what happens if you sin after baptism?

Within the Catholic tradition there are two types of sin: venial and mortal. Full details of what this entails is beyond what we need here; for more see the Catechism of the Catholic Church. In simple terms, a venial sin is a lesser sin that can be readily forgiven through confession and making sufficient restitution, known as penance. A mortal sin is much more serious, often something done intentionally, such as murder, with malice aforethought. A mortal sin nullifies the effect of baptism and puts the soul back into a state of sin. If not redeemed, mortal sin ultimately results in the eternal death of hell. Venial sin, on the other hand, does not result in complete separation from God's grace. It still offends God but does not ultimately deprive the sinner of eternal happiness or result in everlasting damnation, though it does merit some kind of temporal punishment.

Before we look further into this, we should ask if there is any biblical justification for dividing sins up into these two categories. Catholics point to 1 John 5:17, where we read, 'All wrongdoing is sin, and there is sin that does not lead to death.' By implication there is sin that does lead to death, hence mortal sin. Protestants do not agree with this interpretation of the verse. They suggest it means that some sins lead to immediate physical death (such as those of Ananias and Sapphira in Acts chapter 5), but that this is not always the case. In addition, there are no lesser or greater sins when it comes to eternal punishment. All sins deserve the same, and all are forgiven in the same way by repentance and trust in God's grace and mercy.

Likewise, there is a significant difference of views on baptism. Most Protestants regard baptism as being for believers, meaning that it comes after repentance and faith. For Catholics, baptism can occur soon after birth as it then puts that child under 'sanctifying grace', guaranteeing their place in heaven even if they die while young. But this 'sanctifying grace' is forfeited by committing a mortal sin. The only way to regain this is through confession to a priest and subsequent penance. The soul is restored through the merits of Christ's death, but penance is also needed. These acts of penance can take several forms. They usually involve performing good works such as prayer, fasting and giving, but can also require direct acts of restitution, such as apologising and healing any hurts caused. The overall aim is to rectify the wrong done and present a renewed commitment to each other and to God.

As an initial sacrament, baptism removes all possibility of eternal punishment and makes a person fit for heaven. But baptism cannot be repeated, so later sin requires something else. This 'something else' involves confession and penance. Unlike baptism, penance has the advantage of being repeatable, but it is not as powerful as baptism. Penance may take away guilt but it only reduces the punishment for a mortal sin from an eternal one to a temporal one. And venial sins also need to be paid for by penance as they incur temporal punishments. So purgatory has a role to play in both types of sin but what exactly is this role and when is it required?

In general, the eternal punishment of sin can be removed through the sacrament of confession, but the temporal punishment for sins remains even after confession has been made and absolution given. Hence a priest gives the confessing sinner a penance to perform. Through penitential practices, a person works off the temporal punishment for their sins in this life, but if any of this is left unfinished at the end of their life, what then? If this happens, or if there is any venial sin left unconfessed, then any outstanding temporal punishment must be endured in the immediate afterlife before entering heaven. This is done in purgatory, which therefore completes what confession and penance would have achieved if that person had lived long enough. Purgatory takes care of the balance.

So in the Catholic tradition, everyone is either in a state of sanctifying grace or of mortal sin. Those who die in unconfessed mortal sin cannot avoid hell, but those who die in sanctifying grace go to heaven either immediately or eventually via purgatory. But going directly to heaven was very unlikely. You would have to die either straight after baptism, or after confession and completion of the penance required and before committing another venial sin. But, by their nature, venial sins were very common, hence the need for regular confession, so most Catholics expect they will need to be purged to some extent. But what kind of suffering would this entail and for how long?

How much time you would spend in purgatory depended on how much debt there was left to pay, and hence how much purification was needed to become fit for heaven. No-one would want to spend more time in purgatory than was absolutely necessary, so, to reduce the length of time there, the Catholic Church introduced the idea of indulgences. These usually took the form of certain religious acts being performed by others still on earth. So friends and family could do something on your behalf after your death. This often involved giving money, for instance paying for masses to be said on behalf of the deceased or contributing financially towards the latest papal project. It was the latter that caused Luther to begin his protest against indulgences and other practices, and which in effect began what became known as the Reformation.

In addition, in medieval times indulgences were also granted to those who fought in holy wars, especially the Crusades. Taking part in these would guarantee you or your family time off in purgatory. However, as with all indulgences, how much time was subtracted or whether anyone could really tell if this had or had not actually happened was debatable.

In addition to the indulgences mentioned above, the Catholic Church introduced another way of reducing time spent in purgatory, known as 'The Treasury of Merit'. This was an accumulation of credit that had built up over time not only from the merits of Christ himself but also from those of past saints. If someone had been particularly good then a certain amount of merit was left behind at the end of their life. This could be added to this depository for the benefit of others later. Again, it is not clear how these calculations were worked out.

One point to stress is that no amount of merit from this treasury, or indeed from any other indulgences, could reduce in any way at all the punishment for anyone in hell. Another puzzling question in all this is that if someone goes into purgatory for their own good, in particular so that they become fit for heaven, then why would it be thought sensible for them to be bought out early? Do they come out part-purged or enter heaven still unready?

We ought to ask if there are any texts which suggest purgatory is biblically valid. Some point to 1 Corinthians 3:12-15 which talks about being tested by fire and 'escaping through the flames'. But here Paul is referring to fire testing the quality of people's work for the purpose of rewards, not purifying people regarding their sins. Moreover, this takes place on the Day of Judgement rather than over a period of time beforehand, so it doesn't relate to purgatory in any way.

The one passage that is usually referred to as validation of the idea of purgatory is found in the second book of Maccabees, chapter 12, verses 39-45. As many know, this book is in the Apocrypha not the Bible, at least not in the Protestant Bible. However, the Catholic Bible does include the Apocrypha and so for them it is part of the Word of God. The story related in these verses refers to soldiers who had fallen in battle after committing the sin of idolatry. Judas Maccabeus decided to make atonement for them, including prayers for the dead and taking up a collection as a sin offering. He did this believing that, as a result, their sin might be wholly blotted out and thus they might be redeemed from eternal punishment and rise again one day. It is his action on their behalf which, we are told, supports the modern practice of purgatory.

But there are several issues with this. As well as the fact that the books of the Maccabees are not generally regarded as inspired scripture and so not authoritative concerning matters of doctrine, the link between the actions of Judas Maccabeus and the Catholic teaching on purgatory is rather tenuous. What we read in this story says nothing about any period of purgatory or of shortening any stay there. Rather it speaks of a military leader who acted in the light of Old Testament practices in the hope that God, in his mercy, might still grant his dead soldiers life in the world to come. Moreover, this story actually contradicts the doctrine of purgatory as their sin was that of idolatry, which in Catholic terms is a mortal sin not a venial one. To die in an idolatrous state would result in hell, not purgatory.

A final point is that Judas may have believed that his actions would make a difference to the eternal fate of his men, but the story does not say whether or not it did. It does not record the outcome so we have no idea whether or not God accepted what Judas did and was more lenient towards the idolatrous soldiers. It is extremely dubious, therefore, to suggest that this story can provide support for any kind of new doctrine, let alone one as debatable as purgatory.

It is possible that, for some, purgatory may offer some kind of comfort in that if we die not properly fit for heaven then God has provided us with an opportunity to atone in the next life for those things we failed to atone for in this one.

But if this is not biblical then it doesn't provide any real comfort. In fact, it robs us of the certainty that being born again through repentance and faith we go straight into the Lord's presence on death. It also suggests that the finished work of Christ on the cross is not so finished after all. It must be less than effective if we need to add something towards our redemption.

One thing in its favour is that it does take sin seriously. It reminds us that sin has consequences, that we are not to take forgiveness lightly and that repentance may require action of some kind. But the real issue with purgatory is that it is based on, and builds upon, other misunderstandings and errors, such as those concerning the types of sin, the nature of baptism, the initiation of penance and the practice of indulgences, which are effectively ways of buying God's forgiveness. Once you start with an error, then others tend to follow in an attempt to bolster a flawed system. In this case, the final result is a distortion of the biblical message of the cross and forgiveness.

Overall, there is nothing biblical or apostolic about purgatory. It is a church-based tradition which began in the fourth century and gradually developed until, in the twelfth century, it became the doctrine of Purgatory we know today. We should, therefore, dismiss any idea of purgatory when building up our understanding of the afterlife and, in particular, the intermediate state. There are no souls in purgatory as, quite simply, purgatory does not exist. Above all, we should not let this non-biblical tradition contradict what we have already learnt in the last two chapters about *sheol* and *hades*.

In our next chapter we will tackle another tricky topic, that of animals in the afterlife.

Chapter Eleven

Animals in the Afterlife

In this chapter we will consider what happens to animals when they die. Do they continue to exist in any way?

For some people this topic will be among the most sensitive that we will be examining in this book. But we cannot shy away from the more delicate issues that we come across within our general theme of death and the afterlife, so we will be trying, as always, to bring some clarity into such matters by seeing what the Bible has to offer in these cases.

Most of us would say we are animal lovers, especially when it comes to our pets. We lavish love and attention upon them, making sure they are properly fed and well cared for. We want them to have the best life possible and understandably so, as pets often provide joy, solace and companionship, and not just for the elderly or those living alone. As such, it is easy to regard our pets as members of the family. But we must be careful not to blur the distinction between people and animals. Although animals are a wonderful part of God's creation, we must remember that they are not persons.

Nevertheless, a certain amount of emotional attachment can seem natural, and such feelings can easily be enhanced when a pet dies. Their death can be a great loss and some expression of grief is understandable. Pets often show great love, loyalty, even sacrifice, so sorrow at their passing is appropriate. In addition, hopes can then arise of being reunited with them in the afterlife. People often ask with concern about the 'salvation' of their pets. Care is needed over answering such questions. Emotional responses should not take priority over biblical truth.

One reason people may believe in some kind of 'animal heaven' is simply due to a strong desire for it to be true. It brings comfort and provides something positive to say to children who often feel the loss more. A longing for an 'animal heaven', or at least that animals may be part of our future heaven, may be natural but can lead to some wrong thinking. For instance, we might argue that without our pets we will not be happy in heaven so they must be there too. If not, God will have failed to provide real joy for us. But our heavenly pleasure should be focused on God himself, not on any pets we have enjoyed in this life. To think otherwise suggests that our idea of eternal happiness is faulty.

So is there any scriptural basis for animal immortality? To answer this we should start with their creation. What exactly are animals? How are they the same as us? How are they different from us? We looked at this earlier in Chapter Three on the nature of Man so we won't repeat all this here, but here is a brief summary. God made both animals and humans, and described them both as living beings (*nefesh chaya*). Both have a physical component but, in Adam's case, it was when God breathed into him that he became a living being. God didn't do this with animals. Hence, we are in the image of God, animals are not. They cannot know God or relate to him as we can.

So animals and humans differ in respect to what is inside the body. We have an extra dimension, qualities which make us a person. This includes a spiritual element, or soul, which also enables us to survive death and be resurrected later. Animals do not have this, so no part of an animal survives death. There is no continuity of existence for animals in the intermediate state or beyond, and hence there can be no resurrection of existing animals. They have no continuing spirit to put into an immortal animal body. Looking at your pet dog or cat you might think it has a 'spirit' or personality, but this is of a different kind to that of humankind. It is part of how they were created by God but it is purely an element of their animal existence while in this world.

Another difference between animals and humankind is that we think about the possibility, even likelihood, of life after death. We can contemplate eternity and what it might hold for us. There is no evidence that animals consider such things. They may instinctively fear danger or death and have a fight-or-flight response; they may also seem to recognise when one of their own has died and some are even known to mourn. But this does not mean they are consciously aware of their own mortality, the inevitability of death and what might come after. We consider these things because we are made differently.

Genesis tells us that God made the animals lower than humans, and that we are to rule over them (Gen. 1:28).

We might prefer the idea of stewardship rather than dominance, nevertheless this follows from our standing within God's created order. Also, as part of this, Adam was invited to name the animals (Gen. 2:19). God led all the creatures into Adam's presence so he could decide what to call them (presumably a generic name rather than a personal one; horse rather than Dobbin!). We get the impression that God was watching on with interest. What will Adam make of these creatures? Look closely, Adam; see what I have made. In particular Adam was to realise that although animals may be similar to him in certain ways, with some bodily features in common, they were not *of the same kind*. None of them would be a suitable helper, a true companion, or a soul mate. One aim of this parade of animals was to make Adam feel different, special, even alone. This would intensify his desire for a genuine companion, and hence his delight when God created woman, bone of his bones, flesh of his flesh. Here was his true soul mate.

Another difference between humans and animals is that they don't need salvation in the way we do. It was Man who brought sin into the world, not animals. Certainly our sin affects them. They are part of creation that is subjected to frustration, groaning while awaiting our redemption (see Rom. 8:19-22). However, they are not awaiting new bodies of their own. But then, neither will they suffer eternal punishment if they don't repent! We can take comfort that there is no 'doggy hell', for instance.

Salvation in the way we know it simply does not apply to animals. One rather unorthodox view regarding animal 'salvation' was offered by C.S. Lewis in his book *The Problem of Pain*. He thought it possible that 'certain animals may have an immortality, not in themselves, but in the immortality of their masters'. His idea was that just as we are saved in Christ, so pets can be saved in their human masters. They gain eternal life by being part of the household of faith of humans. But there is nothing scriptural about this. It is merely a personal conjecture without any convincing reason to support it.

Turning to scripture, we find an interesting passage in the book of Ecclesiastes. In chapter 3 and verses 19 to 21 we read:

> 'Surely the fate of human beings is like that of the animals; the same fate awaits them both; as one dies, so dies the other. All have the same breath; humans have no advantage over animals. Everything is meaningless. All go to the same place; all come from dust and to dust all return. Who knows if the human spirit rises upward and if the spirit of the animal goes down into the earth?'

In typical questioning fashion, Ecclesiastes, the teacher, is goading his students into thinking more carefully about the fate of humans. Based upon outward appearances, at death we are no different from the animals. We suffer the same fate. An inanimate body is left behind and returns to dust. So is there any advantage in being human? Only if something different happens after death, but 'who knows?' (v21) If this passage is agnostic in tone in order to provoke thought, then at least later on we do get a more positive statement from him regarding humans. In 12:7 we read, 'the dust returns to the ground it came from, and the spirit returns to God who gave it'.

Here the created difference between Man and the animals is pivotal. Man has a God-breathed spirit which returns to him. The animal 'soul' is not God-breathed. It lacks a spiritual dimension so it returns to the earth along with its body. Overall, the elements that God created when forming man and the animals, return to their point of origin, whether dust or God. Animals go back to the earth entirely. They decay and are gone. We return to God with regards to our spirit. From this we conclude there will be no animals in the intermediate period of disembodiment as there is no continuing spirit in their case. However, this does not preclude animals later in the afterlife. It's just that these won't be the same as those who lived before. Instead God can, and probably will, create new animals to take their place. But is there any biblical evidence that this will indeed be the case?

There is a well-known animal passage in Isaiah 11:6-9 which seems to relate to some kind of afterlife, or at least a different kind of life from the one we experience now. This is often incorrectly quoted as 'the lion will lie down with the lamb'. Although this is a good summary, the passage is longer than that and involves more creatures.

These verses state that the wolf will live with the lamb, the leopard will lie down with the goat, the calf and the lion will feed together. It continues that the cow will feed with the bear, their young will lie down together, and the lion will eat straw like the ox. The last bit is repeated later in Isaiah 65:25, an abbreviated version of the above, which states that 'the wolf and the lamb will feed together, and the lion will eat straw like the ox, and dust will be the serpent's food. They will neither harm nor destroy on all my holy mountain'.

The main questions raised about these verses are whether they refer to literal animals, and when exactly this will happen. Some say this is anticipating the new earth mentioned later in Isaiah 65:17 and 66:22, but the more common view is that it points to the Millennium. A clue is the phrase 'in that day' found in the two verses that follow straight after verses 6 to 9. This phrase usually indicates the Messianic age or the age to come, when everything is transformed, harmony replaces enmity and natural ferocity is removed, all in contrast to the present age. We won't attempt here to describe details of the Millennium but this is the most likely context of Isaiah's prophetic statement in these verses. It also fits what it is imagined life on earth will be like under Christ's rule on his return. We should note, however, that if these are literal animals within the Millennium then they are still examples of existing creatures on earth now. They will behave differently but continue to die as normal, rather than automatically be part of the final eternal state. God will create new animals for this.

Some, however, prefer not to regard these as literal physical animals at all but as something figurative. One example is that these are different human personalities who all live together in brotherly love in the Christian age. Once converted to Christ all becomes peace and harmony between men, something we obviously see now. No?

When we turn to the book of Revelation we read of creatures with animal-like features, such as lion, ox and eagle (4:6-9). But like most of Revelation we have to decide how much is symbolic. Certainly the Greek word here for 'creature' is *zoon*, from a word meaning living, the equivalent of the Hebrew word *chayah*, and from which we get zoology and zoo. This Greek word is used elsewhere in the Bible for literal animals, including in the Septuagint version of the Old Testament for animal sacrifices, which were real enough, but this is hardly conclusive proof of real animals in heaven. These passages in Revelation are visionary. John is trying to describe these creatures as they appeared to him in ways he and his readers could understand. For instance, how literally do we take the description of Jesus as a seven-eyed, seven-horned slain lamb (5:6)? Moreover, John's vision is of the intermediate or pre-eternal state, and we have already seen there are no animals there. It is quite possible that these creatures which John observed were more angelic than former earthly animals, but with recognisable features which symbolised something to John. If we want better proof that there will be animals in the eternal state then perhaps we can find one in Revelation 21:5 where God declares, 'I am making everything new!' Surely such a comprehensive restoration means that 'everything' must include animals too.

If there are to be animals in the new earth, some rather curious questions follow. For instance, will we still eat them? We didn't eat meat until after the Flood (Gen. 9:3), and it can also be argued that if animal death was part of the curse due to our sin, then once this curse is lifted animals need no longer die, so presumably we will not eat meat. Moreover, we read that on the new earth 'there will be no more death or mourning or crying or pain' (Rev. 21:4). This doesn't specifically say only human death, so this may well apply to animals also. They too will live forever and enjoy a better life!

Another interesting point is whether in the new earth we will all naturally be able to get much closer to all animals, including lions, sharks, crocodiles and others that currently want to do us harm (or even eat us!). Like Adam in Eden, will we be able to inspect them and see more closely what God has created? Perhaps we will understand God better and worship him more by having close-up contact with this part of his new creation.

We might also ask whether extinct animals will be brought back. If so, will there be dinosaurs in the new earth?! That's an intriguing thought. If they were part of God's original creation of a perfect animal world, then maybe yes, though they might seem a bit out of place among the other animals. But if they were created for his glory, and speak of his awesome power, then why not, though now without their violence and hostility. And if they are not there, then does that mean God made a mistake originally in creating them? Discuss!

We might also wonder if some of the animals in the new earth might still be our pets. As we have said, these won't be exactly the same ones we once had, though God could create new ones to resemble them so that effectively we cannot tell the difference. Maybe he will do this as a good gift to us his children because it would please us, just as an earthly father buys a pet for his child.

Animals may not be as valuable as people but God made them too, and he has touched many people's lives through animals. Humans have always had some kind of attachment with animals ever since Adam named them. Some people devote their whole lives to animals, such as farmers, zookeepers and vets. God intended man and animals to relate so why not again in the new earth? Without animals, Eden wouldn't have been Eden, so why would he not include in the new earth what he provided for our pleasure then? Moreover, if man was told to rule over the animals in Eden then perhaps the new earth will be where we will fulfil this calling, only this time we will be able to do this better as by then we will be fully redeemed from all sin.

There are many biblical texts which show that God cares for animals. For instance, after the Flood he vowed, 'Never again will I destroy all living creatures, as I have done' (Gen. 8:21). He then included them in his covenant with Noah (Gen. 9:9-17). Perhaps we can conclude by saying that the most convincing proof that God will recreate animals for his new earth is not so much that we like them but that he likes them. He will do this for his good pleasure.

In our next chapter we will look at another very demanding and emotive issue, that of the death of babies and infants.

Chapter Twelve

Babies and Infants

In the last chapter we considered what happens to animals when they die. If that was an emotive issue then how much more that of babies and infants! But we cannot ignore this completely. Even if evidence for our conclusions proves to be a little more elusive than we might like, then we can at least aim to tread along a biblical path towards those conclusions, and along the way remove some wrong ideas and straighten out our thinking a little.

Inevitably there is great grief when a little one dies. Questions are bound to be asked as to why a life has been taken so soon, before it has had chance to develop, and contribute towards the family and humanity in general. Even if a child has been part of a family's love for a while, its death is still difficult to come to terms with. Such a short time on earth seems to make it even more cruel. Perhaps parents may turn to God at such times of loss but equally it may turn them away from God, even destroying any faith they once had.

The issue of the death of infants and babies, including miscarriages and stillbirths, should never be treated merely as a matter of theological curiosity. There is too much at stake emotionally. Sensitivity is required. Usually theologians and Bible teachers like to claim certainty in what they teach, and people do tend to expect their pastors to be able to provide answers to all their problems and needs! But if scripture says little it is best not to try and fill in the gaps with dogmatic answers of our own.

Some may not like this lack of clarity and want to accuse God of not keeping us sufficiently informed. And what do we tell unbelievers who might be deterred from the Christian faith if we can't help them in this matter? But the fact is there aren't any biblical texts that tell us specifically about the fate of those who die as a baby or infant.

Even though there are no definitive scriptures we may still be able to find clues within the overall tenor of scripture and what we know about the nature of God. On this basis many argue that those who die young will have a place in the world to come. Historically, Christianity has generally embraced this view. But if this is true we should still state clearly that this is not because they are innocent or without sin.

When assessing the likelihood of infant salvation we cannot ignore the doctrine of original sin. There are no exceptions to the verses in Romans which declare that all have sinned and fall short of the glory of God, and that as a result death comes to us all (Rom. 3:23, 5:12). Babies and young children may be relatively innocent compared to adults, simply because they have had less chance, if any, to commit acts of sin, but their inherited sin nature still needs redemption. They might be less guilty than adults, as indeed some adults might be less guilty than other adults, but less guilty is not the same as innocence. Original sin is still sin and requires Christ's atoning work, the sole provision by which God's wrath is satisfied and eternal life is granted.

We cannot ignore or bypass the doctrine of original sin just because someone is below a certain age. We cannot, for instance, claim that God may allow a certain limit of sins and if infants haven't reached that yet then they are 'saved'. Nor can we assert that babies start 'saved' and continue as such until they reach a certain age when their sin starts to take effect. What would this age be? Would it be the same for everyone? Similarly, the view that personal faith is not required for those too young to believe, again makes us wonder at what age such faith does become necessary? None of these ideas provide a satisfactory resolution of the issue we are discussing.

A more sensible suggestion may be that God knows how each new baby would have responded to the gospel later in life and whether they would have repented, and so he can determine their salvation (or otherwise) on that basis. This might appeal to some, but again without any clear scriptures on this we should not be dogmatic.

It is also important to realise that we cannot say, 'Of course God saves young children.' There is no 'of course' in such matters. Simply being young at the time of death does not mean that God must save them. Nor can we condemn God as unfair if he doesn't. Salvation is always a gift, given by grace. Babies may look innocent but in biblical terms they are not sinless and need salvation in the same way as anyone else, through Christ and his death on our behalf.

We saw in a previous chapter that the Catholic doctrine of infant baptism claims to provide 'sanctifying grace' for a baby and so guarantees a place in heaven if they die soon after. However, this is purely a later church tradition which started long after the New Testament was written, with the first explicit mention around AD 220. It became a more universal practice within the Catholic Church by AD 400 and therefore does not feature in anything Christ or the apostles taught.

Another theological speculation within the Catholic tradition is that of limbo, or more precisely 'Limbo of the Infants' (*limbus infantium*). This is a supposed place of bliss where the souls of children go if they die without having received baptism. The argument goes that they are unable to enter heaven as they are not free from original sin, but they are too young to have committed actual sins and so do not warrant punishment. This state of limbo is therefore supposedly permanent, though some within Catholicism hope that these infants may still attain heaven eventually rather than remain in limbo forever, but the Catholic tradition provides no certainty over this.

We mentioned earlier there are no specific texts on this matter of the afterlife of young children, but that maybe there are clues within the overall tenor of scripture and the nature of God. We will look at some of these next.

2 Samuel 12:15-23 is one of the most quoted passages on this matter. One consequence of David's sin with Bathsheba is the death of the child after seven days. David was distressed and others thought it might result in him harming himself, but the opposite was the case. David fasted and wept while there was still chance of the child living, but afterwards he

reverted to normal life. In verse 23 David says, 'But now that he is dead, why should I go on fasting? Can I bring him back again? I will go to him, but he will not return to me.'

It is the last sentence here that is the key one. Some argue it implies the child has gone to heaven, or at least David believes so, as he says, 'I will go to him', and presumably David is expecting a heavenly future for himself. This is pinning a lot on one short statement. At best it provides a hint. But does David really mean this, that he will see him again in the afterlife? The other option, indeed the more likely one, is that David is saying that he himself will someday meet the same fate. 'I will go to him' is more naturally interpreted as 'go the way of all flesh' or, simply, 'I will die'. We also need to remember that in David's time the immediate afterlife was *sheol*. So we should not read into this passage a later, more developed, view of the afterlife. Maybe David is stating that when he dies he will meet this child in *sheol*, and that he is correct in this, but we cannot use this to deduce anything about what we now think of as heaven.

Overall, there is no great clarity from this passage, and we would wish for something more assuring and less open to textual criticism. So are there any other texts that are more illuminating?

People often point to what we know about how God relates to babies and also to Jesus' attitude towards young children. There are several interesting texts to help us here.

For instance, David, in one of his psalms, states: 'Yet you brought me out of the womb; you made me trust in you, even at my mother's breast. From birth I was cast on you; from my mother's womb you have been my God' (Ps. 22:9-10).

In addition, Jeremiah heard from God that, 'Before I formed you in the womb I knew you, before you were born I set you apart' (Jer. 1:5).

Paul records something similar about himself in Galatians 1:15, 'But when God, who set me apart from my mother's womb . . .'

And then there was the occasion when an angel informed Zechariah, the father of John the Baptist, that his child 'will be filled with the Holy Spirit even before he is born' (Luke 1:15).

This is all very encouraging and informative, though it could be noted that these were all exceptional people who were destined to have a special purpose within God's plans, and that therefore none of them died young! So perhaps again we cannot generalise too much from these texts.

When it comes to Jesus' attitude towards little children there are some well-known passages, in particular Matthew 18:1-14 and 19:13-15 (cf Mark 10:13-16; Luke 18:15-17). Again these are informative and encouraging, and offer some hope for their salvation: 'For the kingdom of heaven belongs to such as these' (Matt. 19:14). But the main point of Jesus' teaching here is how adults need to emulate childlike characteristics, especially humility and trust, if they are to enter the kingdom of heaven. Also, Matthew 18:6 suggests these little ones ('those who believe in me') are already old enough to have faith in Jesus in some way, though it isn't clear if this is personal trust or some other kind of belief in him, such as Messiah or prophet.

The passage in Matthew chapter 18 goes on to say that these little ones have personal angels assigned to them, often called guardian angels, who 'always see the face of my Father in heaven' (v10). But nothing more is said about their role. Do they keep these little ones close to God's heart? Does this mean God saves them in a way which may override the usual way of salvation for adults? Some would argue from these verses that this may be so, but then at what age does this end? We certainly learn that the 'Father in heaven is not willing that any of these little ones should perish' (v14), but isn't that so of everyone?

From all this, and more, we can willingly accept that those who die as babies and infants will have a place in God's eternal plan. But, as we saw with animals in the last chapter, other tricky questions then emerge. For instance, what kind of new bodies will they have, and what age will they be in eternity? We would say that for adults we can assume some continuity between our old and new bodies. But for infants and babies their bodies never had chance to grow and develop. One view, not substantiated in any way, is that babies and infants will be resurrected as they were at death and then grow up as they would have done in their natural life. This would enable their parents, if they are also resurrected, to have a chance to hold them as children and see them grow into maturity. Sentiment may be getting in the way of reality here, but certainly we could expect that a child in heaven will eventually be complete, with the full mental and physical capabilities they would have known.

Of course the matter of our age in the eternal state applies to all of us anyway, not just the very young. If we die at six, sixty or one hundred and six, is it likely we will be that age forever? One view is that thirty is the adult age of perfection so we will all be that age, even if we never made it that far in life. Thomas Aquinas, a medieval Catholic theologian, preferred the age of thirty-three, perhaps largely based on the presumed age of Christ at death. Science may concur with this figure as apparently before that age we have not reached our optimal development from a functional perspective; after this we are in decline! It seems the idea that deterioration begins at this age is based on DNA, so if the blueprint for our glorified body is in our old one somehow (through our DNA), then we may suppose that our new bodies will be resurrected at that optimal age and stay like that.

However, this could be boringly monotonous if we are all the same age forever so another idea is that we appear ageless in heaven. In effect, age won't apply any more in the way it does now on earth, so in heaven no one appears to be a particular age. It may even be possible for us to reflect different ages of our previous life at various times as we wish, perhaps according to whom we meet. All this seems very strange and is obviously pure speculation, though perhaps possible if our new body is made rather differently from the body we have now.

When thinking about animals in the afterlife, we looked at Isaiah 11:6-9. Verse 6, which talks about various animals lying down next to each other or feeding together, ends by saying 'and a little child will lead them'. There are further references to children in verse 8: 'The infant will play near the cobra's den, and the young child will put its hand into the viper's nest.' We mentioned in the last chapter that this is more likely referring to the Millennium than the eternal state, in which case these will be children who are still growing up.

In conclusion, this particular aspect of the afterlife has left us with many unanswered, even unanswerable, questions. For instance, we may be consoled by the thought that the outcome of all baby deaths, including miscarriages and stillbirths, is that they go directly into God's presence. But this may leave us wondering what then happens to aborted babies. How would we face the question: what's so wrong with abortion then, if they go straight to heaven?

Hopefully, despite all these remaining complexities, our investigation has given us much that seems plausible or worth thinking over further. It is not all uncertainty. We can be sure that we have a loving God who doesn't want anyone to perish, so it is reasonable to conclude there is a way for a baby or young child to be saved for God. And that way will be on the same basis as for the rest of us, the sacrificial death of Christ. Surely we can trust that the Father will have covered the deaths of our children through the death of his own Son?

And, ultimately, that is what it comes down to, trusting in the fairness of God. As part of the Adamic race these little ones will be judged, but we can echo the words of Abraham, 'Will not the Judge of all the earth do right?' (Gen. 18:25). We can be sure that our loving heavenly Father always acts with perfect justice. In this way we can give comfort and hope to anyone who has suffered the loss of a child, even if we can't provide definite statements. In the end, as in many things, we leave it with God and have faith in him. The souls of children must simply be entrusted to the mercy of God.

In our next chapter we will look at communicating with the dead, whether we can and whether we should.

Chapter Thirteen

Communicating with the Dead

In this chapter we tackle the contentious subject of communicating with the dead. There are several important Bible passages which shed light on this topic but, before we look at these, we will start by asking three simple questions regarding communication with the dead. Is it possible? Is it desirable? Is it permissible?

Recent surveys show that many people nowadays tend to think that communicating with the dead is at least possible. This view is gaining support. But can you actually do so? Could it conceivably be real, rather than deception or a fraud perpetrated for various reasons? We have seen earlier that the spirits of those who have died are not in some kind of soul sleep but are conscious and active. They also retain certain personal attributes. They are still the person they once were, even though now disembodied. On that basis we might say communication with them is possible, or at least we cannot rule it out completely. However, death is defined as total separation from everyone on earth and from everything going on there, which suggests any kind of communication or contact between the dead and the living should be difficult, if not impossible.

In our chapter on *hades* we looked at the story in Luke chapter 16 about Lazarus and the rich man, both of whom were in the realm of the dead. There was communication between them, or at least between the rich man and Abraham, but we are also told there was a great chasm between them. So what about between the dead and the living? The rich man clearly thought such communication could take place as he wanted to send Lazarus back to earth to warn his brothers. It is interesting that he wasn't told this was impossible, just that it would be fruitless. No-one would listen or repent as a result.

If it is possible to communicate with the dead, then why might it be thought desirable? For some this might be emotionally attractive. They miss the personal contact and think that talking with someone they once loved will bring comfort. But would that really be so? The rich man in Luke chapter 16 had a good reason to want to send Lazarus back, namely to warn his family. But would they have liked what they heard? Usually those who do try and communicate with the dead expect to hear nice things. But what if that isn't the case?

Another possible reason for desiring to communicate with the dead is curiosity. After all, it is our future too. We are all going that way one day, so why not attempt to get some correct information ahead of time from those who really know? It is because of such desires and longings that we must ask our third question, whether communicating with the dead is permissible. Does God allow this?

In the Bible we find that God consistently and strongly condemns all such activity. It is both offensive to him and harmful to us. Several texts indicate this, in particular three in Leviticus.

Leviticus 19:31 states, 'Do not turn to mediums or seek out spiritists, for you will be defiled by them. I am the LORD your God.' Then in Leviticus 20:6 we read, 'I will set my face against anyone who turns to mediums and spiritists to prostitute themselves by following them, and I will cut them off from their people.' Later in that same chapter, in verse 27, we have, 'A man or woman who is a medium or spiritist among you must be put to death. You are to stone them; their blood will be on their own heads.'

There are several points to take from these verses. Firstly, even trying to communicate with the dead is dangerous. It defiles us. Secondly, those who practise such matters are to be dealt with severely and, thirdly, anyone who turns to such people for their 'services' are opposing God and will suffer spiritual consequences. To underline all this, God emphasises his lordship over his people. 'I am the LORD your God.' These are commands not suggestions.

These texts demonstrate the seriousness of such matters but also give an indication that these practices did take place. Mediums and spiritists were common among pagan peoples and so God warned Israel, prior to their entry into Canaan, that they must not imitate 'the detestable ways of the nations there' (Deut. 18:9). These detestable ways included all kinds of occult practices such as divination, sorcery and consulting the dead. In all these things God commands his people to be blameless before him (Deut. 18:9-13). One person who disregarded these commands was Manasseh, one of Israel's most evil kings. He followed 'the detestable practices of the nations', 'practised divination, sought omens, and consulted mediums and spiritists'. As a result he aroused the anger of the Lord (2 Kgs 21:2, 6).

We notice two words in these texts: mediums and spiritists (today we might say spiritualists). These are two separate words in Hebrew but with similar meanings. One is *ob*, which is derived from someone who mumbles or speaks from another place. This is similar to how a ventriloquist entertains us by 'speaking from his stomach' to make it appear that his dummy is engaging in conversation with him. But we are not fooled by this, whereas such 'mumbling' from a medium can be highly deceptive. Interestingly, this Hebrew word also carries the idea of speaking from within the ground or from the inside of an empty bottle or water skin.

The other Hebrew word is *yidoni*, from *yada* meaning 'to know intimately'. This is sometimes referred to as a 'familiar spirit', often found in older translations such as the King James Version. The idea behind the word is that of a regular acquaintance in the spirit world, well known to the medium who therefore has a ready and willing contact they can call on whenever needed, like you would a friend or neighbour. Such easy access and loyal friendship guarantees the provision and accuracy of any knowledge sought, and correct answers to any questions asked. At least that is the intended impression.

In each case, the aim is to make us think we are hearing from someone now dead when it may be from another source entirely. It could be deliberate fraud on the part of the medium who makes a living out of such practices. Such instances have occurred and are well documented. Or, more seriously, it could be demonic in origin. Demons, or evil spirits, can impersonate a dead person based upon detailed knowledge of their life in order to create an illusion of genuine communication. They can even mimic a voice, personality and physical appearance. They often talk of love and peace, and include favourable references to God or Christ, all to convince us that what we hear is authentic. But to try and contact the dead is to invite fellowship with the forces of darkness who, while pretending to be helpful, are actually damaging your soul. Any so-called knowledge gained from such contact is at best unreliable and at worst misleading. We cannot learn about life after death from those whose purpose is to confuse and deceive. As we have said repeatedly, the only reliable information we have is found in the Bible and we cannot supplement this from elsewhere.

Any discussion on contacting the dead has to take into account the famous passage where Saul visits the so-called 'witch' of Endor in order to consult with the spirit of the prophet Samuel. Doesn't this show the Bible condones such things? But what actually happened? Was this genuine? We will look at this now, in 1 Samuel 28:3-25.

We notice at the start of the story that Saul was very much afraid on account of an impending battle against the Philistine army camped nearby. Indeed, 'terror filled his heart' (v5). How would this battle play out? What should he do? The usual means of enquiring of the Lord (dreams, the High Priest's use of the Urim, or prophetic words) had produced no results, so in a state of panic, Saul turned to an alternative way of deciding what to do. But, as we shall see, this provided him with neither the guidance he was seeking, nor relief from his fears. In fact, by the end he was in even worse shape.

Previously, Saul had done the right thing in expelling the mediums and spiritists from the land (v3) but now he decides he needs one! He has to ask his attendants to find one for him as there weren't supposed to be any left, but it seems one remained in a tiny village called Endor (v7). So Saul set off at night in disguise. After all, why would you want to be recognised as the king who had forbidden such things and who was now going against his own ruling?

Clearly the disguise worked, as the medium didn't recognise him. Suspecting a trap, or at least fearing for her life, she at first refused his request to 'consult a spirit for me . . . and bring up the one I name' (v8). Saul swears to her by the Lord that she won't be punished for this, so she agrees and asks whom she should bring up. Samuel!

From this point on, this already strange story develops in an even more bizarre way. We are not told if the medium had actually begun her customary way of operating. Quite possibly she hadn't. But she suddenly sees something and it spooks her, so to speak! She cries out in terror, not just because she now realises it is the king who has consulted her but because this is not what she would have expected.

Instead of making contact with her 'familiar spirit' who would pretend to be Samuel and speak through her, she sees an actual spirit (or 'shade') coming up out of the earth (*sheol*). When she describes him as old and wearing a robe, Saul recognises this is indeed Samuel. And then rather than this spirit making utterances through her, Samuel and Saul speak to each other directly. They engage in a conversation totally without her involvement. This is not how these things were meant to happen! What is going on?

This is unlikely to have been a demonic manifestation otherwise the narrative would have made it clear. Nor was it fraud on the part of the medium as she was shocked and terrified and not in control of circumstances. More likely this was a genuine event in which God allowed Samuel to make contact with Saul. Here is God taking charge of the situation, hijacking it for his own purposes, namely to bring a message to Saul that God wanted him to hear. Moreover, this was not to be the sort of pleasant and agreeable message which a 'familiar spirit' might usually give through a medium. Rather this was a prophetic word of judgement.

As one of Israel's most respected and reliable prophets, Samuel had anointed Saul as King and ministered to him in the early years of his reign. Now he was about to tell him something that would devastate him. God had indeed departed from him, as Saul himself had stated (v15). In fact, it was worse. The Lord had become his enemy. God had torn the kingdom out of Saul's hands and given it to David, and now the Lord was going to deliver him over to the Philistines. Saul would be defeated in battle and die as a result. 'Tomorrow you and your sons will be with me' (v19) is telling Saul that he will soon be joining him in *sheol*, the realm of the dead. If Saul wanted further chats with Samuel, he wouldn't have to wait too long! And indeed this soon came true. Critically wounded in battle, he took his own life rather than allowing himself to be captured or abused by the enemy (see 1 Sam. chapter 31, also 1 Chron. chapter 10). His three sons perished too, as predicted, as did many Israelites as they fled from the Philistines.

When he heard this message from Samuel, Saul fell to the floor, filled with fear. If he was seeking relief from his fears, then this hadn't worked. Far from it. He ends up even worse. His strength had left him and now he knew the fate that awaited him.

Whatever you make of the details of this story and whether you agree this was God bringing Samuel back into this world for his own purposes in dealing with Saul, it is obviously not a scenario for us to repeat or even think of repeating. If this is what communicating with the dead is like, then the result is hardly positive or reassuring. Avoid at all costs! And if God is allowing this to happen in this instance, then it does not imply he is now endorsing what he previously prohibited.

Before we leave this story, we ought to think about the form in which Samuel appeared. It was not a resurrection. He was not in his final new body. Rather this was Samuel in a disembodied state, but perhaps in a temporary visible form with certain physical features which made him recognisable, though it isn't clear how simply being described as old and wearing a robe was sufficient in this respect.

The same question could be asked of the other example in scripture where dead people appear on earth, namely Moses and Elijah at the time of the transfiguration of Jesus (Matt. 17:1-8). Again, they were not being resurrected at this point, but were evidently recognisable, even by Peter, James and John, who had never met them before!

One view concerning what others saw is that Samuel, Moses and Elijah materialised into our physical world. But in the case of Moses and Elijah the Greek word for 'appeared' simply means in some way they became visible (Matt. 17:3). So the other view is that God was peeling back the curtain into the world of the afterlife, similar to when Elisha asked God to open his servant's eyes so he could have a momentary glimpse of the spiritual realm around them (2 Kgs 6:17). So in this way of understanding the passage, Samuel, Moses and Elijah were seen as they currently exist in the intermediate state rather than taking on a new form here.

Either way, we may not be sure how Moses and Elijah arrived at the scene of the transfiguration, but it definitely wasn't because Jesus summoned them up. He was being transfigured when they just turned up! So, as with Samuel, it seems it was at God's own initiative that Moses and Elijah appeared on earth and for his own specific purposes. Certainly, there is no evidence the disciples afterwards thought this was a good idea and should try it themselves sometime.

We conclude that neither Samuel nor Moses and Elijah were raised up in the way prohibited elsewhere in scripture, so these incidents cannot be used to contradict these texts. And if it was God himself who brought about such contact between the dead and the living, these were particular and isolated occasions, and do not indicate it was normal for him, let alone legitimate for us to try and imitate.

We end this chapter with some advice from Isaiah 8:19-20. 'When someone tells you to consult mediums and spiritists, who whisper and mutter, should not a people enquire of their God? Why consult the dead on behalf of the living? Consult God's instruction and the testimony of warning.' Wise words indeed.

In our next chapter we will ask if there is any chance after death to hear the gospel and receive salvation, a topic usually referred to as post-mortem evangelism.

Chapter Fourteen

Post-Mortem Evangelism

In this chapter we will consider the idea that there is an opportunity for repentance and conversion after death. This view states that you can still hear the gospel and be saved even after you have left your body and entered the intermediate state of the afterlife. Salvation thus remains a possibility for those who have died, or at least for some of them. Is this in any way biblical or is it just wishful thinking?

Within Christian tradition it is usually taught that someone's eternal destiny is settled by the time of their death, but there has always been a small minority who have differed over this, proposing that conversion is possible in the next life. This idea goes under the label of 'post-mortem evangelism' or sometimes 'post-mortem encounter' as this can only happen through some kind of encounter with Christ in the afterlife. There are several variations of this basic proposition.

One is that this is only for those who never had a 'first chance' to hear the gospel during their earthly life. This version is known as 'the universality of the first chance', as everyone eventually hears the gospel at some point, if not before they die then afterwards. This is a popular idea if only because it promotes a fairer view of God. No-one will perish purely out of ignorance or lack of opportunity. It can also be used to explain how babies who die can still 'go to heaven', a topic we explored in an earlier chapter. Under this idea, the spirit of the baby is told the gospel message in the afterlife and will be saved, or otherwise, according to their response then. Again, the popularity of this is based upon fairness and an overall sense of God's justice.

Another version of post-mortem evangelism says that even if you heard the message of salvation during your lifetime but rejected it, there may still be an opportunity to hear it again in the afterlife and change your mind. In other words, you are offered a 'second chance'.

An even more extreme version teaches that those in hell may also be given a chance to repent and 'get a transfer' to heaven. This is close to the doctrine of universalism in which, ultimately, everyone gets to heaven. However, it is not totally the same as proponents of this version of post-mortem evangelism say each individual in the afterlife still has free will and so may continue to reject the offer of salvation, though it is difficult to see why anyone would once they realise exactly what is at stake. Another point is that this version presumes that hell follows immediately after death, which is not the case. Hell is part of the final state, not the intermediate state, and follows the final judgement, after which there is no question of any change.

It is easy to understand why post-mortem conversion has its attractions. It resolves various issues such as those concerning the death of babies and infants, and those who didn't have any chance to hear the gospel during their lifetime. Moreover, in all these variations, post-mortem converts are still saved by the death of Christ so it can be argued that this doesn't contradict how we normally view the method of salvation, just the timing of it.

But we cannot define our doctrine on what may feel good and right to us. Instead we must look at what the biblical texts say. Are they in favour of this idea or against it? For some, there are several texts which prove that post-mortem conversion is a valid doctrine, but whether these actually do prove this is open to debate. Meanwhile, other texts are adamant this cannot happen. We will look at these first.

The obvious starting point is the story of Lazarus and the rich man in Luke chapter 16 which we have looked at before. Verse 26 tells of the 'great chasm' set in place to prevent any crossing between *hades* and Abraham's side in either direction. Some may argue this is just a story whose main point lies in our attitude towards wealth and so should not be taken literally in respect of other matters. As such it does not define doctrine regarding our final destiny. Yet any story can teach more than one truth, and even if the main truth here is about money, it is unlikely Jesus would put this in a false setting if he believed any transfer between post-mortem realms was possible. Overall, we can conclude that this passage does indeed teach the permanence of one's fate after death and thus it removes any possibility of post-mortem conversion.

Hebrews 9:27 states that 'people are destined to die once, and after that to face judgement'. This can be read as saying that we go straight from one to the other without any time between for anything, let alone conversion. However, 'after that' does not necessarily imply straightaway. It just records a relative order between events. So for some this verse does not conclusively rule out the possibility of post-mortem salvation, but it is generally thought that there is enough of a clue here to suggest we are judged according to our standing before God at the time we die.

As for those texts which may suggest that post-mortem salvation is possible, we can quickly deal with Revelation 21:25. Here it says the gates of the New Jerusalem are never shut. Some argue this is to allow the entry of late converts, but this is totally invalid. Not only are we now in the eternal state, after the final judgement, when all fates have been settled, but the point of the verse is that, unlike earthly cities where the gates are closed at sundown to prevent invaders, this isn't needed with the New Jerusalem as there 'will be no night there'.

Another key point in this debate centres on John 5:25 where Jesus says, 'A time is coming and has now come when the dead will hear the voice of the Son of God and those who hear will live.' For some, this verse suggests that at least some of those who are dead will hear the voice of Jesus and become saved. But there is no indication here what Jesus is saying to them. There is no reason to assume he is giving them the message of the gospel so they can make a decision for him. Moreover, if the phrase 'the dead' refers to all the dead, which seems most likely, then this would suggest universalism, which is the idea that everyone gets to heaven in some way by the end.

Part of the debate over this verse is whether these are the physical dead or just those considered to be spiritually dead. In verse 24 Jesus has mentioned those who have already crossed from death to life in a spiritual sense because they have heard his word and believed. So might he be adding in the next verse that this will also be the case for everyone eventually? It is actually more likely that the real meaning is found slightly later in verses 28 and 29 which clarifies the context.

In verses 28 to 29 Jesus states that 'a time is coming when all who are in their graves will hear his voice and come out – those who have done what is good will rise to live, and those who have done what is evil will rise to be condemned'. This refers to resurrection and judgement in the future, not conversion in the intermediate state of the afterlife. Jesus is looking ahead to a day when everybody hears his voice as he calls them out of their graves to discover their eternal fate. This may be reminiscent of Jesus calling in a loud voice, 'Lazarus, come out!', at which point Lazarus emerges from his tomb, though as this is not his actual resurrection into a new body, perhaps a better comparison is found in 1 Thessalonians 4:16 where Paul writes about Jesus' return. 'For the Lord himself will come down from heaven, with a loud command . . . and the dead in Christ will rise first.'

Overall, it is difficult to sustain that John 5:25 confirms post-mortem evangelism in any way. So we will turn next to the passage which proponents say proves their case more than any other.

1 Peter 3:18-20 records a curious episode in the post-death but pre-resurrection life of Jesus. We read that, 'He was put to death in the body but made alive in the Spirit. After being made alive, he went and made proclamation to the imprisoned spirits – to those who were disobedient long

ago when God waited patiently in the days of Noah while the ark was being built.'

This raises many questions. What was this proclamation? Was it the gospel of redemption? And who exactly are these imprisoned spirits?

Then later in the same letter, in 4:6, we read, 'For this reason the gospel was preached even to those who are now dead . . .' Does this add anything to our understanding of post-mortem evangelism?

Jesus spent a short period of about three days in a disembodied state between his death and resurrection. Peter seems to suggest in his letter that for at least part of that time Jesus went into the realm of departed spirits and communicated with other spirits there. Was this to preach the gospel to them? To give them a chance to be saved?

There are two points to make about these verses. Firstly, Jesus only made proclamation to those who had lived during a certain time in history, namely 'in the days of Noah while the ark was being built'. This was a particularly wicked time (Gen. 6:5-7), and rightly they are described as 'disobedient'. This was the generation who refused the message of Noah, a preacher of righteousness (2 Pet. 2:5), and his warnings to repent, and so were completely wiped out in the flood. Did that mean they deserved a 'second chance'? And why only them and not others, or even all sinners? Even if we agree there is some form of post-mortem evangelism in these verses, there is nothing here that allows us to generalise to everyone or even anyone else. From this we cannot infer such opportunities are offered now or even that it has happened at any time since. What is being described is a one-off action in the past which applied to a limited number.

But was this an offer of salvation at all? The crucial second point is that the Greek word in 3:19 for 'made proclamation' is *ekeiruyxen*, which simply means to announce or declare. Earlier translations, such as the King James Version or even the New King James Version, translate this as 'preached', which is misleading as, to our minds, this usually implies preaching the gospel. But to preach can simply mean to proclaim any kind of message. It could equally be one of condemnation or judgement. Jesus may be proclaiming his victory over sin but at the same time reinforcing their punishment, the very opposite of a second chance. There is no escape for these imprisoned spirits. They are staying where they are. Furthermore, even if Jesus was preaching the gospel to them, there is no mention of any positive response, so we can hardly regard this as successful post-mortem evangelism.

Turning to 1 Peter 4:6, we do now have the Greek word for preach (*eueingelisthei*) and mention of the gospel. But it does not say it was Christ who preached the gospel, something which is required in post-mortem evangelism, as it is an encounter with Christ that changes things. More significantly, Peter writes that the gospel was preached to those who are *now* dead, not that the gospel is *now* preached to those who are dead. In other words, he refers to those who are dead at the time he was writing but who heard and embraced the gospel while still alive. So this text, like all others, cannot be said to uphold that a 'second chance' salvation is taught by scripture.

Given that the passage in 1 Peter 3:18-20 is rather obscure it is no surprise there have been many attempts to explain it. One is that Jesus went down to *hades* to release the souls of those who had lived by faith in Old Testament times. After all, if Jesus is now offering paradise to New Covenant believers, starting with the thief on the cross, then shouldn't those who had been faithful within the old covenants join them? His redemptive work now done, Jesus can release them into a better kind of afterlife while awaiting the final resurrection. But this ignores the fact that the passage refers only to those living in Noah's day and that they were disobedient, not faithful, so such an interpretation is not valid from these verses.

Another view is that Jesus himself came to earth during the time of Noah, in a pre-incarnated or spirit form, to preach to the unbelieving people living on earth then. They are referred to as imprisoned spirits in this passage as this is what they now are for refusing his message at that time. Others go even further and suggest that Jesus was preaching *through* Noah. It may have been Noah's voice but he was just the human instrument that God used to communicate his message. So in one sense it was Christ preaching, but not directly. But this contradicts what Peter writes about Jesus having been put to death and then made alive again, which places it clearly in his post-death, pre-resurrection period not in an earlier time frame, so this view cannot be taken too seriously either.

And then others debate whether these are human spirits at all. Some suggest these are the spirits of the Nephilim who contributed towards the evil during the time of Noah (Gen. 6:1-4) or maybe even the fallen angels already imprisoned by God (2 Pet. 2:4, Jude 6). The details behind all this are beyond the scope of this book but even in these cases there is no evangelisation or second chance on offer.

Before we end this chapter we should mention that many will have heard that Jesus 'descended into hell' because it is part of a creed. For instance, the Apostles' Creed states that 'he suffered under Pontius Pilate; was crucified, dead and buried; he descended into hell; the third day he rose from the dead'. There is something similar in the later Athanasian Creed. But creeds do not determine doctrine. They may be valuable but are not authoritative like scripture. Moreover, the phrase 'he descended into hell' was not in the original Apostles' Creed which developed over time. It was not written by the apostles themselves nor by a single church council soon after. The creed took shape over centuries and only in later versions did the phrase start to appear with many accompanying problems.

As before, 'hell' is not the right word; *hades* would be better. Some taught it must refer to his hell-like suffering on the cross as he was abandoned by the Father, but the phrase was specifically placed after 'buried' and before 'raised from the dead' so it cannot point to the cross. Many sought a meaning within 1 Peter 3:18-20 as we have been discussing. A new phrase then emerged, 'The Harrowing of Hell', to denote the triumphant descent of Christ to plunder hell and bring salvation to souls held captive there since time began. He took these pre-Christ believers to be with him in paradise. We have already dismissed this from our study of this passage. Moreover, no creed says he descended into hell in order to liberate or save the dead, but the harrowing of hell became common in medieval imagery, art, poems and sermons, all based more on imagination than anything biblical or anything that made much sense.

What Jesus did go through in those three days without a body may remain a bit of a mystery, but it is clear it does not involve him preaching the gospel or anybody being saved as a result.

Our exploration of the afterlife has taken us into some difficult territory in which we have encountered some bumpy terrain. We now head towards the twin topics of resurrection and judgement, starting in our next chapter with the resurrection of Jesus.

Chapter Fifteen

The Resurrection of Jesus

We now begin our consideration of the topic of resurrection, and where better to start than with the resurrection of Jesus himself?

John chapter 11 contains one of Jesus' great 'I am' statements. In verse 25 he declares, 'I am the resurrection and the life.' The context is the recent death of Lazarus, a dear friend and brother to Mary and Martha in Bethany near Jerusalem. Jesus arrives there to find Lazarus has been in the tomb for four days, but undeterred by this he calls him out and brings him back to life. This is not a resurrection into a new body but a return to this life in the same body. He will die again. The same can be said of similar miracles in the Bible, such as those performed by Elijah and Elisha in the Old Testament, and by Peter and Paul in Acts, as well as by Jesus in the gospels, namely the widow of Nain's son and Jairus' daughter. But in the case of Lazarus, Jesus makes his remarkable statement about resurrection which, unlike his other 'I am' statements (vine, light, bread and so on) is not part of a general discourse but part of a dialogue between Jesus and Martha.

In verse 21 Martha declares that if only Jesus had been there with them, he could have prevented Lazarus from dying, an accusation perhaps made out of grief and sorrow. Jesus replies, in verse 23, by stating that her brother will rise again, which may have been intended to provoke Martha into a discussion and get her to verbalise her faith on this matter. So what did Martha believe about resurrection, and how typical was this at the time? How had the Old Testament informed her thinking and Jewish expectation in general on this matter?

Martha states her belief quite clearly. 'I know he [Lazarus] will rise again in the resurrection at the last day' (John 11:24). Notice she refers to *the* resurrection that will occur *at the last day*, meaning at the end of the age. There was a range of views about resurrection within first-century Judaism, with some not believing in it at all. Martha seems to stand within the conventional belief that there will indeed be a new bodily existence of some kind when God has put all things right and defeated evil. At which point the messianic kingdom can begin and, as part of this, the righteous will be raised to live again.

Within mainstream Judaism, the Pharisees concurred with this understanding while the Sadducees did not. They dissented not just because bodily resurrection seemed absurd but because there were no examples of this, or indeed any indication of this, within the Torah which was the only part of the Hebrew scriptures that they accepted as authoritative. For them, there was no afterlife to look forward to, and all rewards were to be found in this world and this life.

If the Sadducees had looked beyond the first five books of the Old Testament would they have found anything to convince them of a possible future resurrection? Certainly there is nothing much to suggest a well-developed doctrine but a couple of texts do stand out. One is Isaiah 26:19 which states, 'But your dead will live, LORD; their bodies will rise – let those who dwell in the dust wake up and shout for joy.' The other example is found in the later text of Daniel 12:2, 'Multitudes who sleep in the dust of the earth will awake: some to everlasting life, others to shame and everlasting contempt.' This is the only place in the Old Testament where the phrase 'everlasting life' (*chayey olam*) occurs which may suggest something new is being presented here. However, a question is often raised over the word 'multitudes', which typically means 'many' or a 'large number', not everyone. So what happens to everyone else?

Moving into the literature of the intertestamental period, the second book of Maccabees describes the martyrdom of seven Jewish brothers at the hand of Antiochus Epiphanes (2 Macc. chapter 7). The second and fourth brothers affirm their hope of resurrection (vv9, 14), while the third displays an expectation that his body will be fully restored at the end (v11). Their mother also adds her hope for their resurrection which she assumes will be physical (vv23, 29).

Returning to Martha, we notice that Jesus does not contradict her assumption about an end-of-age resurrection, but he does qualify it by personalising it to himself with his 'I am' statement. He also adds 'and the life', emphasising that resurrection is a means to an end, namely everlasting life for those who believe in him.

As for the resurrection of Jesus himself, we must start with his death and what happened immediately afterwards. Scripture records that just before he breathed his last, Jesus committed his spirit into the hands of the Father (Luke 23:46). He left his broken body on the cross for others to bury, while his spirit remained active for whatever purpose the Father willed. We saw in an earlier chapter that Jesus did not descend into hell or plunder it in order to rescue souls, but being disembodied he would have gone into the realm of departed spirits, something he referred to as being in paradise (Luke 23:43), a term reminiscent of the Garden of Eden (cf Rev. 2:7). As he offers paradise to the dying thief on the cross beside him, we can understand this as being part of *hades* where other disembodied spirits would also be. We can also equate this with Abraham's side or bosom in Luke 16:22.

Meanwhile, Jesus' body remained out of sight, ready for something remarkable that was about to happen. But what exactly?

We start with something Jesus said to his disciples just after his transfiguration. As they came down the mountain, he ordered them not to tell anyone what they had just witnessed until the Son of Man had 'risen from the dead'. They did indeed keep quiet on this but couldn't help discussing among themselves what this 'rising from the dead' actually meant (Mark 9:9-10). Why such a discussion? Did they not understand resurrection in the same way as Martha and others?

The reason lies in the wording used. In verse 9 the Greek is *ek nekron anastei* (had risen from the dead) and later in verse 10 it is *ek nekron anastenai* (rising from the dead).

Nekron, meaning 'dead', is familiar to us from necromancy (communicating with the dead, a topic we looked at earlier) and necropolis (city of the dead, basically a large cemetery). We may also recognise the words for 'risen' and 'rising' as Anastasia is a girl's name, meaning 'resurrection'. But there is also the crucial tiny word '*ek*' similar to the Latin '*ex*', meaning 'out', as in exit. The whole phrase, therefore, refers to Jesus rising *out from among the dead*, or to give it even more emphasis, he was predicting he would be *out-resurrected out from among the dead.*

Here was a totally new idea. Jesus would not be raised along with everyone else at the end of the age. Rather, he would be resurrected before then, leaving the realm of the dead earlier than anyone else. As such, he would be the first to be raised from the dead, ahead of others and ahead of the expected time. A sort of pre-resurrection resurrection. This would change everything and explains why the disciples discussed what they had just heard Jesus say.

This new idea of being 'out-resurrected out from among the dead' became part of the apostles' preaching, not just to refer to Christ's resurrection but also to those who believe in him and who will be raised to life by him. This phrase was now used regarding the future resurrection of believers, though never of the ungodly. For instance, in Philippians 3:11 Paul refers to believers attaining to the 'resurrection from the dead' (*ekanastasin ton nekron*). And in Acts 4:2 the apostles proclaimed 'the resurrection from among the dead', not just 'of the dead' as in an end-time event. We will return to this later as it helps resolve questions concerning the future resurrection.

Meanwhile, we must tackle one of the main issues regarding the resurrection of Jesus, namely the nature of his new body. To what extent was it the same as his old one? How did it differ? This is worth trying to understand as one day our new bodies will be like his glorious body (Phil. 3:21; 1 Cor. 15:49), something for a later chapter.

Among the several mystifying aspects of Jesus' post-resurrection appearances is whether or not he was easily recognisable. At his first appearance, by the garden tomb, it took Mary Magdalene a while to realise it was Jesus standing nearby. Reasons usually given for this are that it was barely daylight and she had been crying, but perhaps more significantly is that she wasn't expecting anything like this. However, eventually voice recognition took effect as she heard him say her name and full realisation soon followed (John 20:14-16).

It took longer for the two disciples on the Emmaus road to realise who their companion was. On the journey they were somehow kept from identifying him. It was only when he broke bread with them some time later that their eyes were opened and they recognised him (Luke 24:16, 31). At which point he disappeared from their sight!

At other times the disciples recognised him at once, though at first they needed convincing he was not a ghost or spirit (Luke 24:37-39). Eventually, they came to realise there was a considerable degree of continuity between the physical man who had walked on earth with them and the person they experienced now. He ate with them (Luke 24:42-43), cooked breakfast for them (John 21:9-14), and could be touched (Matt. 28:9; John 20:27). Incidentally, it is often wondered why Thomas was allowed to touch Jesus but

Mary Magdalene was not (John 20:17). But in this verse the Greek word (*aptou*) is not 'touch' but 'hold on to' or 'cling'. 'Stop clinging to me' would be an apt translation. Perhaps she was clasping his feet or giving him a hug! Either way, she is reluctant to let go. So Jesus is not forbidding any kind of contact, just that kind and at that moment. He gives two reasons for this. One is that he has not yet ascended to the Father; the other is that she has to go and tell others he is alive and about to ascend to the Father (John 20:17). Obviously, this is not the ascension we read about in Acts chapter 1, which occurs 40 days later. But what Jesus is saying here suggests he had only just received his new body and that this had occurred here on earth, in the garden, not in the heavenly places. Now that he was re-embodied, his first task was to return to the Father in this form. It is not mentioned here why this should be, and any speculation on this can be left to others.

One feature of Jesus' new body is that it could display the marks of his crucifixion, or at least some of them. Thomas had doubted that the other disciples had seen the Lord alive and needed proof for himself. Jesus appeared a week later and showed him the nail marks in his hands and the hole in his side from the spear (see John 19:34, 20:24-27). We may wonder why other disciples, such as those on the Emmaus road, hadn't noticed these before, especially his hands. Were these not obvious all the time? Perhaps you had to look closely or ask. And what about other aspects of his passion? His back had been flogged to shreds, his forehead pierced with thorns and his feet also nailed. There is no mention of these regarding his new body so although Jesus manifested certain marks of his suffering on this one occasion, perhaps they were not on regular display.

In fact, would we really expect such physical damage and mutilation from the past to be a continual part of the resurrected life of glory and perfection?

It is often mentioned that Jesus' new body defied the laws of physics in that he could walk through walls or doors. This is based on the two occasions when the disciples were in a locked room, once when Thomas was absent and later when he was there with them (John 20:19-29). However, this is to misread the text. Nowhere does it say Jesus did this. Rather, he simply appeared inside the room. The text does not say Jesus was outside in the first place and that because he couldn't get in in the usual way he just walked through the door! He simply 'came and stood among them' (John 20:19, 26). Perhaps a resurrected body can pass through solid objects, but this is not part of the biblical text here despite it being commonly taken for granted. Instead, it seems he could materialise at will, making himself visible and tangible whenever he wanted. This certainly transcends the normal laws of physical existence. The risen Christ is no longer bound by such limitations. His new body is a real physical body, clearly identifiable, but with new properties and so could operate differently. Incidentally, when Jesus appeared the second time he clearly knew about Thomas' doubts and what he had said previously. This was a lesson for all the disciples. It's like he's still here even when he's not! No wonder Thomas worshipped him.

We have reached one final question. Was Jesus' new body exactly the same as his old one, just transformed, or was it something totally new? In other words, did Jesus re-enter his old body within the tomb which then began to breathe again, at which point he simply walked out of the tomb (not through it; the stone had been rolled aside!)? Or did his old body supernaturally disappear in some way, decaying quickly and disintegrating back into nothing while he was re-clothed with a totally new version, outside the tomb, within the garden?

There are arguments either way. For some the empty tomb proves that his resurrected body was the same as the one that died on the cross. Moreover, when in John 2:19 Jesus said, 'Destroy this temple, and I will raise *it* again in three days' (italics mine), he was referring to his body, and so '*it*' must mean the one he had then. Or was this just an analogy? Would you really rebuild a temple with the same stones or fashion a new one out of other material, similar but not the same?

For some a one-to-one correspondence between his old and new bodies is indisputable. Certainly there was a correspondence but how direct? Jesus referred to his new body as having flesh and bones (Luke 24:39). Were these the same as before? Today we might ask if his risen body had the same DNA as his old one. If so, his resurrection did not negate his genetic tie to his ancestors. He thus remains a descendant of Abraham and of David. He is still of Abraham's seed, and 'of the tribe of Judah, the Root of David' (see Rev. 5:5). In fact, his claim to the throne of David and future rulership in the Millennium and beyond depends in part on this. In short, the risen Jesus remains fully human, related to Adam, and in particular he is still Jewish.

The resurrection of Jesus is a fact of history. It happened at a specific time and place on earth. Yet it is far more than just another historical event. Its meaning surpasses all others. Jesus didn't just come *back* to life, he went *forward* into life, a new kind of life. This was not a return to the same existence, as with Lazarus. The resurrection of Jesus was as significant as the creation of the universe because it was the start of a new creation. Paul refers to Christ's resurrection as 'firstfruits' (1 Cor. 15:20, 23), based upon the Jewish feast which occurred three days after Passover. Jesus was the first to be raised in this way, before the end of time and as the start of a new creation which would guarantee our future resurrection. He has been raised ahead of us. Resurrection is our goal too! Some of what we have learnt about Jesus' resurrection and new life will help us understand our own to come, which we will start to explore in our next chapter.

Chapter Sixteen

The Resurrection of the Body

In the last chapter we looked at the resurrection of Jesus, and we follow it up now by considering our own future resurrection as believers in him. There are several key issues within this topic. One is the nature of our new body. Another is when our resurrection will occur and the related matter of how many different resurrections there will be. It will take us two chapters to cover all this.

The resurrection of the body is foundational to the Christian faith yet it remains controversial. Evidence suggests it cannot happen. Dead means dead, with no return to life. To believe otherwise is to invite scorn or ridicule. So it is common to deny a physical resurrection, preferring instead to believe in the immortality of a non-material soul. As we saw in an earlier chapter, the influence of Greek thinking, especially Platonism, leads us in that direction. Our soul is trapped in a body and must escape, never to return to anything similar. But a bodiless resurrection contradicts its essential meaning, so it is critical that we assert the truth of a physical resurrection and try to understand as much as we can about this from the biblical texts.

We start by affirming that for believers in Jesus, resurrection is both certain and necessary. Certain because Christ himself has been raised as our firstfruits. As we read in 1 Corinthians chapter 15, 'each in turn: Christ, the firstfruits; then, when he comes, those who belong to him' (1 Cor. 15:23, cf v20). Paul, on trial before Agrippa, declared that the Messiah was 'the first to rise from the dead' (Acts 26:23), implying that others would follow. Then, writing to believers at Corinth, he states clearly that 'by his power God raised the Lord from the dead, and he will raise us also' (1 Cor. 6:14), and again, 'we know that the one who raised the Lord Jesus from the dead will also raise us' (2 Cor. 4:14). Moreover, several times Jesus spoke of raising up on the last day those that the Father had given him (John 6:39, 40, 44, 54).

The resurrection of the body is also necessary for several reasons. One is that if we are to spend eternity with Jesus, we should have a body as he does. Moreover, in the beginning Man was created as a spiritual and physical unity. This was part of God's original good plan and remains his intention for us, so we cannot be disembodied spirits forever. In particular, resurrection is the reversal of death and indicative of its ultimate defeat, so the separation of body and soul which occurs at death must be undone. Another reason bodily resurrection is necessary is due to the future environment in which resurrected people will live, namely a new heaven and a new earth. Despite what people are often taught, or have assumed, from Greek-based thinking, our final destiny is not in some vague ethereal realm but in a renewed physical creation. It must be stressed that a correct understanding of bodily resurrection requires us to see it within the larger concept of cosmic redemption, the completion of which is a new heaven and earth. It is here that we will serve and glorify God forever. Logically, a new heaven and earth must be repopulated somehow, which necessitates the resurrection of individual bodies.

Once we accept that resurrection is both certain and necessary we must then grapple with questions concerning the nature of our new body and its continuity with our old one, as we did regarding Jesus in our last chapter. Within the New Testament the most extended treatment of this topic is found in 1 Corinthians chapter 15. It seems the early Christians in Corinth struggled somewhat with the idea of a physical resurrection and asked the same basic questions, perhaps because of their background in Greek thinking. Paul starts by tackling those who were denying a future bodily resurrection at all (1 Cor. 15:12ff). He establishes that our resurrection is guaranteed because of that of Jesus as our firstfruits, as we have mentioned earlier.

Then from verse 35 onwards Paul addresses practical objections to the dead being raised. 'How are the dead raised? With what kind of body will they come?' (v35). To rephrase this slightly, how will God actually do this? What similarities can we expect between our old bodies and our new ones? Will they be exactly the same, or just similar? Will there be some continuity or be entirely different? We tackled such questions regarding Jesus in our last chapter and now we must address the same with respect to our own resurrection.

The view that our new body is exactly the same as the one which died is very common and features in some of the great Anglican declarations of faith. The Westminster

Larger Catechism (1647) states, 'The self-same bodies of the dead which are laid in the grave, being then again united to their souls forever, shall be raised up by the power of Christ.' The Westminster Confession agrees: 'All the dead shall be raised up with the self-same bodies, *and none other*' (italics mine), though it does add 'with different qualities'.

But what might 'self-same' actually mean? The same collection of particles that we have now? The argument that our new body will be reconstituted from exactly the same atoms is what causes many to discount a physical resurrection. And with good reason. After death the body decomposes back into the ground. It may then enter the food chain and be eaten by animals who are then eaten by humans. Indeed occasionally, some parts of corpses are eaten by animals anyway. In such cases, the particles which once made up our body may well over time become part of a different human body. Incidentally, cannibalism is a quicker, more grotesque version of this! But whether you are buried or cremated, whether you die naturally, in a fire, or at sea, in the end your body is going to disappear back into the earth, maybe over centuries, maybe sooner. In fact, most human bodies throughout history, or at least significant parts of them, no longer exist. The cells that once made them up have been dissipated across the world in many different ways. So if we are to expect exactly the same body at resurrection then what is known as the 'ownership of atoms' becomes a real issue. How will God handle that? Does he have to sort out some kind of complex biological jigsaw to put us back together again? Does he have to seek out every little bit of dust that we once were? We can understand how this becomes a significant objection to a physical resurrection but, as we shall see, this is not how things are going to happen so we don't have to defend this rather unrealistic scenario.

Another problem with the identical body theory is that we don't have a single set of atoms throughout the whole of our lives. Our body is a constantly shifting collection of cells as some die and are replaced by others. So if God is to reassemble all the same particles, is it those we have at the time of our death, or in the prime of life, or at some other time? Any of these have been as much part of our body as at any other time. No single collection of particles defines our physical identity. This is not really how we think about our body anyway. We see it as a unified whole but which changes over time. So the idea that God will gather up all the particles of our old body and reassemble them into our new body such that every atom will once again be joined to those it knew before, is not one that we have to justify in order to support the truth of a physical resurrection.

Instead we can refer to what Paul taught in 1 Corinthians 15:36-44. Here he uses the simple but very effective analogy of a seed being sown and raised. This demonstrates both continuity and differences. The resulting plant has an organic connection to the seed. It naturally follows from the seed, and the seed contains everything the plant is going to be, but such continuity does not make them identical, at least not in terms of containing precisely the same particles.

This illustration of a seed negates the view that God reassembles every atom of our old body when presenting us with a new one. All the particles in the seed do not become part of the plant, and many in the plant were not present in the original seed. Hence, not every particle of your body that is sown at death has to become part of your new body when it is raised. God can create your new body to be like your old body without having all the same atoms.

Paul's use in these verses of the repeated phrases 'it is sown' and 'it is raised' has led some to believe that this 'it' that is raised must be identical in molecular terms to the 'it' that is sown, but this is to press the grammatical construction too far. This does, however, stress the continuity between our old and new bodies, especially as what follows in each case are the differences between the two: perishable, imperishable; dishonour, glory; weakness, power;natural, spiritual.

We now see, in verse 44, that Paul is talking about a natural body and a spiritual body, which needs further explanation. The Greek words are *psuchikon* (natural) and *pneumatikon* (spiritual). These words, with their *-ikon* endings, are not telling us what each body is made of, but how it operates or what controls it. The natural body is controlled by fleshly desires. It operates according to our senses and the world around us. At present our fallen human nature dominates the way our body acts or wants to act. By contrast, our new spiritual body will function according to God's spirit within us, as by then our spirit will have been made perfect by him. Our glorified body will be totally spirit-led and operate according to a different set of principles.

What is important to realise is that a spiritual body is no less a body. It is not something totally spiritual that happens to be called a body. There is no such thing as a non-corporeal body, and the use of the word 'spiritual' does not negate the usual meaning of the word 'body'. Paul did not say 'it is sown a natural body, it is raised a spirit'. What Paul is describing here is not the material aspects of the old and new bodies but the power that animates them. A spiritual body will most of the time appear and act like a physical body that we are familiar with, though maybe with some extra capabilities and characteristics that are beyond what we are used to now.

Another comment is needed regarding what Paul says in 1 Corinthians 15:50, that 'flesh and blood cannot inherit the kingdom of God'. Here it may seem Paul is discounting any kind of physical body. But the phrase 'flesh and blood' is an idiom within Hebrew thinking for humans as they are now in their natural sinful ways. It was used in contrast to the Almighty God, as when Jesus said to Peter that revelation about his messiahship had not come by 'flesh and blood', meaning human sources, but by the Father in heaven (Matt. 16:17). Paul's argument here in 1 Corinthians 15 is that our 'flesh and blood' nature must be changed before we can enter the eternal state of God's kingdom to come.

At death we undergo one change but remain the same person. We will undergo another change at our resurrection but also remain the same person. There is an element of continuity all through these stages. Some of that continuity will be between our old and new bodies, perhaps by some kind of genetic link, maybe the same DNA. If God created all things without any atoms to start with, then he will have no difficulty in recreating us, and indeed the whole cosmos, in a way such that we will be clearly and recognisably the same 'us'.

But the main continuity comes from our spirit or soul, what we saw earlier is called our *nefesh*. It is this *nefesh* within us that currently maintains our body, so when it leaves the body at death, our body starts to fall apart and decay. Meanwhile, our spirit manages both the continuity and fluctuations in our current bodies as they change over the years. And it is our spirit that can provide continuity between our old and new bodies. In due course, we will experience a second body, but we have just one spirit at all times. At the time of death, our spirit continues and, if we have been born again, it will be re-embodied and continue to direct our new life within a new body.

To sum up, the relationship of our old body to our new body is like that of a seed to a plant. A seed is small and simple yet it grows into something more complex, more glorious. The resulting plant cannot be less than the seed, but it can be much more. Our new body will not be physicality minus but physicality plus, and when we eventually get it and see it in all its glory we will recognise it as coming from the previous body we once knew.

God created the world in such a way that we are constantly surrounded by examples of how our future resurrection will work. Seeds are sown and die, then new life emerges. We can be amazed at this. When we look at an acorn and an oak tree at the same time we might ask in wonder, how did that happen? We may say the same when we get our new bodies.

There are many different kinds of body within creation. Not just human bodies but also animals, birds, fish, even heavenly bodies. Each are of their own kind, and with their own kind of splendour (1 Cor. 15:38-41). God is able to produce new bodies for every current 'seed' body, all according to their kind and each at least as splendid as before.

Overall, we can say that we need not worry about our individual component atoms or how we will die or what might happen to our body immediately after death. Any doubts about our future resurrection probably stem from a lack of faith in God as our creator. Without this faith it can be difficult to sustain belief in resurrection. We look at our current bodies, made from the dust of the ground and which will return to the same. We can't see beyond this. But our immortal bodies have a more glorious origin. Just as we now bear the image of the earthly man, Adam, so one day we will bear the image of the heavenly man, Jesus (1 Cor. 15:49). And it is by the same power that raised Jesus from the dead that our natural body will germinate into our new spiritual one.

In the next chapter we will look at when this will happen and also whether there will be more than one time when resurrection happens. As part of this we must include the resurrection of those who don't believe in Jesus.

Chapter Seventeen

The Timing of the Resurrection

We have been considering the topic of resurrection and, in particular, the nature of the new body we will receive. Now we turn to when this might happen and whether there will be more than one occasion when resurrections will occur.

It may seem strange to even imagine there might be more than one resurrection as it is usual to think merely in terms of a single general resurrection on the last day when everyone will be raised. But is it that straightforward? This matter becomes more complicated in the light of the many theories of how God will bring the current age to an end. Various end-time theologies have produced different answers to this question, so we will have to delve into this to some extent. In addition, the topic of resurrection also relates to that of judgement, which will occupy us in the next two chapters, so there will be some overlap at this point.

We saw earlier how a typical view in first-century Judaism was that of a single resurrection at the last day, as articulated by Martha in John 11:24. This made sense from what little the Old Testament scriptures had to offer. The idea of resurrection was not yet as well developed as it would become after the resurrection of Jesus, together with an expectation of his soon return. It would take more revelation to clarify such matters, including that from Jesus himself in the book we call Revelation. We will look at this and other New Testament texts shortly, but first a brief summary of some aspects of end-time theology as it impinges on our topic. We start by defining terms.

The Millennium refers to the period of time during which Jesus reigns on earth with his saints after his return and before the final judgement. The derivation of the word 'millennium' suggests this will last for a thousand years, though it could just be symbolic of a very long period. Those who believe in this are called Premillennialists, the prefix 'pre-' referring to Jesus returning *before* the Millennium starts. Those who don't believe this will happen at all are described as Amillennialists, where the Greek prefix 'a-' means 'not'. Postmillennialists do believe in a Millennium but one where believers are currently reigning on earth without Jesus being present. He reigns in heaven while we reign on earth on his behalf. For Postmillennialists, Christ returns at the *end* of this period, in other words *after* the Millennium has occurred, hence the prefix 'post'. In this case the Millennium cannot be a literal thousand years as it has already lasted nearly two millennia. It is just a very long period of time.

As part of all this there is also something called the 'rapture'. This is based upon 1 Thessalonians 4:16-17 which describes how the Lord himself comes down from heaven with a loud command, the voice of the archangel and the trumpet call of God, at which point the dead in Christ will rise first and then those still alive on earth will be 'caught up' (raptured) to join them all in the air. There are, of course, several variations of all these main ideas, but this is sufficient for our purposes regarding the stages of resurrection, how many and when.

Both Amillennialism and Postmillennialism require only one resurrection which is for everyone at the end of the age when Jesus returns. We then go straight into judgement and the eternal state. However, Premillennialism needs two separate resurrections, a thousand years apart: one for believers at the start of the Millennium and one for everyone else at the end of the Millennium. It is obvious that believers returning to earth to reign with Christ must become embodied again at this point. Moreover, it should also be fairly clear that this resurrection at the start of the Millennium cannot be a general resurrection of all the dead, as unbelievers will not reign with Jesus during the Millennium.

In simple terms there are essentially two kinds of resurrection: one to eternal life; one to eternal death and damnation. The question is whether these occur at the same time or are separated (by the Millennium). We should add at this point that unbelievers will also be resurrected in new bodies but these will not be glorified like that of Christ, as they will not be spending eternity with him.

We will turn now to some biblical texts to see how they back up these conjectures. Some will imply two resurrections, others just one, though we need to be careful here since the latter may not necessarily mean at a single point in time. There could be a time gap not mentioned in the text. It is possible to talk about resurrection as though it was a single event and ignore any time gaps, especially if this occurs within a general teaching on the topic which is not aiming to be that specific in every aspect.

We start in Revelation chapter 20, which seems to settle matters straightaway! In verses 4 and 5 we read about the 'first resurrection', that of those who come to life and reign with Christ for a thousand years, while the rest of the dead do not come to life until the thousand years are ended. This supports two stages. If there was only one it wouldn't use the term 'first resurrection'. Moreover, a specific time gap is explicitly mentioned, after which the rest of the dead are raised, which we might therefore refer to as a second resurrection.

Although it is clear that those raised in the first resurrection must be believers, debate remains whether this is all believers over the whole of history or just those who remained faithful to Jesus during the time of the antichrist, referred to as the beast, and who were martyred as a result (v4). But just because these martyrs are the only ones mentioned at this point, it doesn't mean that all other believers are not also among those described in verse 6 as being blessed and holy and who share in the first resurrection. We may need other texts to determine this.

While we said earlier that Revelation chapter 20 seems to settle matters in favour of two stages of resurrection, for some this is not the case. They argue that this is the only place in scripture where two stages are explicitly mentioned and too much should not be built upon a couple of verses, especially if it requires a literal view of something, namely the Millennium, in what is a highly symbolic book. They say that the correct approach is to interpret these verses in the light of other texts which provide something more definitive. So let's see what else the New Testament has to offer and, in particular, whether there is anything which contradicts what we have found in Revelation chapter 20.

In John 5:28-29 Jesus states, 'For a time is coming when all who are in their graves will hear his voice and come out – those who have done good will rise to live, and those who have done what is evil will rise to be condemned.' By 'his voice' Jesus is referring to himself, they will hear the voice of the Son of God (v25). Certainly these verses indicate two separate outcomes, life and condemnation, but it is through the phrase '*a* time is coming' that many feel it is suggesting that all this happens at one and the same time.

Rather than 'a time is coming', some translations have 'the hour is coming' which accurately reflects the Greek. But both are equally acceptable. Either way what we have here is a figure of speech, not sixty particular minutes, and one that is often used about the end times without being specific about duration or exactly when. So to say 'a time is coming' when referring to two or more events doesn't necessarily mean they will all happen together at a single moment in time. It is just a phrase indicating generally that this is going to happen. It's coming, maybe not all at once. We might get one part, then another later. So the actual wording is not that conclusive and still allows for two stages. In fact, it seems that Jesus' intention here is to proclaim the universality of resurrection rather than any timings at which various aspects of it may take place. We should therefore be wary of saying this proves just one stage of resurrection for all and so contradicts what we find in Revelation chapter 20.

There is something similar in Acts 24:15, where Paul expresses his belief that 'there will be a resurrection of both the righteous and the wicked'. Again, the use of the words '*a* resurrection' may suggest a single resurrection of both the righteous and the wicked at the same time. Certainly the word '*anastasin*' used for resurrection is singular but, again, there could be a time gap which Paul is not mentioning here as it is not relevant to his main argument. However, some would question whether two resurrections a thousand years apart can actually be called *a* resurrection. Is a two-part resurrection still a single resurrection?

As we have seen before, 1 Corinthians chapter 15 is a key chapter on resurrection. Here Paul writes that Christ will be raised first and then, when he comes, those who belong to him (v23). There is no mention here about those who don't belong to him, when they will be raised. Paul says nothing about unbelievers in this passage, but then why would he when his main aim is to tell Christians about their resurrection? However, Paul does seem to be suggesting an order here: first Christ, then believers, with the implication that unbelievers are raised later. But for some this is an argument based on silence – what isn't said rather than what is – and so doesn't prove anything regarding two stages of resurrection.

Another key passage is in 1 Thessalonians 4:14-16, where again Paul asserts that Jesus died and rose again, and that when he returns he will bring with him 'those that have fallen asleep in him', also referred to a little later in the passage as 'the dead in Christ'. These are clearly believers who are returning with him, and so will need a new body at this point. The main issue here is the use of the word 'first', as in 'the dead in Christ will rise first'. It should be pointed out this is not the same as the 'first resurrection' of Revelation chapter 20. In 1 Thessalonians chapter 4 the distinction is not between believers and unbelievers but between believers still alive and believers already dead. Those who have died will rise before (but only just before) those still alive on earth who are then caught up to meet him and them in the air (v17). This is known as the rapture from the Latin word for 'caught up'.

Here, as in 1 Corinthians chapter 15, we note that Paul is teaching Christians about their resurrection. In particular he is answering their specific question about believers who have died, providing assurance that they will not miss out. So it is not surprising that Paul does not mention unbelievers here. Any idea of their resurrection at a later time is left silently running in the background.

When believers alive on earth at the time of Jesus' return are 'caught up' to meet him in the air, this is not technically a resurrection. They won't have experienced death as such, nor been disembodied in the intermediate state, so they are not being raised from the dead. But they will still receive a new body and be changed in what Paul calls 'a flash, in the twinkling of an eye, at the last trumpet' (1 Cor. 15:52). This leaves one other group, namely those who become believers during the Millennium. Some may die during that period, others may still be alive by the end. When do they get their new body? Perhaps at conversion (possible, though this seems unlikely), or maybe there will be another stage of resurrection for them just before the very end? There is no clear answer to this, so we will not enter into speculation. Here is something else to leave with God. But we can be sure that he is faithful and true, and that they will not miss out.

Can we draw any definite conclusions from all these scriptures or are we left permanently debating whether there is just one resurrection or two separate stages? Here are some final thoughts.

Firstly, we recall what we said in an earlier chapter about Jesus being out-resurrected out from among the dead, and that the same is then taught and promised for believers. We will also be raised out from among the dead, *ekanastasin ton nekron* (Phil. 3:11, also Acts 4:2). This clearly means two stages: believers first, then unbelievers later. You can't be raised out from among the dead if there are no dead left. One day the wicked will also be raised. There is not so much detail in scripture about the nature of their new body. It will still be a physical body of some kind, otherwise it is not a resurrection, but it won't be glorified or like Christ's in any way. We shouldn't speculate too much on this as the Bible reveals very little, though we will need to look at this further in a later chapter on the fate of the wicked.

So from this, it seems as though Revelation chapter 20 with its two stages can be regarded as accurate and other texts agree with this, or at least don't definitely disagree, even if a time gap is not specifically mentioned. We should also note the obvious fact that Paul did not have the book of Revelation when he was writing to Christian churches. It came much later. And as a later revelation, it is possible for the book of Revelation to add more detail, including extending time elements and creating a gap, without contradicting anything previously. If instead it had reduced two stages to one, then that would be more of a problem.

Incidentally, to discount a literal millennium on the basis of it being merely symbolic is also to reject Old Testament prophecies concerning the messianic age, as the book of Revelation is typically building its millennium teaching on what has gone before, adding certain details in the light of Christ. Ignoring the Millennium involves replacing Hebraic ideas with those of Greek-based philosophy, as we have mentioned before. But unlike the Greeks with their disdain of things physical, we can look forward to being clothed in a physical body that has been transformed and is immortal, and reigning with Christ in his kingdom on earth.

We end this chapter by noticing that in Hebrews 6:1-2 the writer speaks about moving beyond certain elementary teachings and into maturity. One of the six areas he mentions is resurrection. An elementary teaching! Perhaps he means fundamental rather than easy! But hopefully by now this topic has become at least a little less difficult to understand. Meanwhile, the final one in his list of six elementary teachings is eternal judgement, so we will explore this in our next two chapters.

Chapter Eighteen

Judgement and the Great White Throne

In our last few chapters we have looked at the topic of resurrection. Now we move on to that of judgement, another key aspect of the Bible's teaching on death and the afterlife, and one which cannot be isolated from others, such as resurrection and the Millennium. Again, this will take two chapters to cover such a large topic in sufficient detail.

Just as everyone will be resurrected at some point, so everyone will stand before God in judgement. This in itself is not so controversial, but there is a lot of debate over the timing, nature and purpose of such judgement. Or is it judgements? Again we must ask, will there be more than one? We will face the same questions we tackled in our recent chapters on resurrection. In addition, when it comes to judgement we now have to examine the role that works will play. That they will play some role is indisputable. Many New Testament texts speak of this or point in that direction. So how can we be justified by faith yet on the last day be judged according to works?

In this chapter we will start with an overview of the topic of judgement and then focus on one particular passage, Revelation 20:11-15, known as the Great White Throne or final judgement.

In our discussion of the resurrection of the body we began by asserting that this was both certain and necessary. It is the same with judgement. Certain, because, as the writer to the Hebrews makes clear, man is appointed to die once and after that to face judgement (Heb. 9:27). Just as death is inevitable, so is judgement, as we see in many other texts, such as Acts 17:31, 2 Corinthians 5:10 and 1 Peter 4:5.

Nor can we argue that judgement is restricted to the Old Testament and not carried through into the New with Jesus. His ministry revolves around the idea of judgement to come at the end of the age. Moreover, God has already appointed Jesus to be our judge, and will not go back on that (see Acts 10:42, 17:31; John 5:22). Whether we relish that thought or not, we have no say in the matter.

Many people may view judgement in negative terms. They feel threatened or worried by it. What might it be like? Here is a big unknown. It may be one of the main reasons why people fear death. After all, if death is oblivion and our body simply rots away, then what is there to worry about? Fear of death often stems from a dread of what may come after. Do we meet our maker? Will we have to give an account of ourselves? Have we been good enough?

Others may simply sneer at the thought of a final judgement. They dismiss it as irrelevant or ridiculous these days. After all, God can no longer be thought of as Creator, and if he is not our maker then who is he to judge us? It is, therefore, common to conclude that judgement will never happen. It is just a myth, they say, an empty threat to keep us obedient and make us conform to certain rules. But, no, it is certain, inevitable, unavoidable. And we should make it part of our preaching and teaching, despite the reaction we might get.

In one sense, judgement is a neutral concept, and not all judgements in the Bible are negative or relating to punishment. They can be encouraging or rewarding. In particular, Christians need not fear judgement. Our sins and failures are dealt with by Christ's death. For us, judgement is an evaluation of the authentic worth of our lives at the end, an assessment of the work of God in us and through us.

We now turn to why judgement, and in particular a final judgement, is necessary. There are several good reasons for this as the intended purpose of judgement is multi-faceted. The two main reasons are obviously to avenge evil and reward good, but there is more behind each of these than just punishments and rewards.

One principle that underlies the need for a final universal judgement is accountability. We are moral creatures, and we have been given free will. We make choices throughout our lives, so there must be consequences. Some of these will occur during our lifetime, but others will not. So before the eternal state can begin, there has to be a final reckoning for all moral creatures (angels as well as men and women). This present age must come to an appropriate conclusion and, as part of this, God must demand an account of everything that has been done, said, and even thought.

Another purpose behind the final judgement is to reveal God's true character, in particular that he is just and fair. At the final judgement, God's sovereignty and righteous judgements will be made clear to everyone, which is why it must be public and involve everyone who has ever lived. We will all then know that he has been totally fair to everyone, and this will resound to his praise and glory throughout eternity. By this means, God will glorify himself by showing how magnificent are his ways, how great is his mercy and justice.

Moreover, a final judgement brings a sense of completeness. After this there will be no need for further judgements to come. Justice by then will be complete. Nothing will have been forgotten or omitted. There can be no cause for future complaints. We can enter eternity knowing everything has been put right. We will worship God forever because we will have seen his final justice at work and our sense of a need for justice will have been satisfied once and for all.

Knowing there will be a final judgement of this kind should affect how we live now. For instance, to live in the realisation that God is the final judge in all things may prevent us seeking personal revenge now and make us more forgiving towards those who have wronged us. It also provides a strong motive for faithful living now, for this is how as believers we will be judged. This is the basis for rewards, which we will mention again later in this book. New believers in Christ should be taught clearly from the start of their Christian life that what they do from now on does matter, and will be taken into account in the final judgement. Anyone heard any sermons on that?

The Bible describes two types of judgements. Some are temporal. They take place all the time and within time. They are often linked to the choices we make in life, and serve a purpose confined to the present. But there is also a final 'Day of Judgement'. Many biblical texts back this up, but this is a figure of speech rather than a literal 24 hours. Nor should we think of this in terms of a typical court scene as we find within our legal system. Although useful as an analogy, this is not a trial as such. Imagine having to queue up with billions of others for your 'day in court'! The final Day of Judgement is not an investigative trial, assessing all the evidence and coming to a decision. By then the verdict is already known. This is more like the final part of the trial, when the sentence is passed, and our final destiny is assigned.

We will now look at one passage which describes this Day of Judgement. This is in Revelation 20:11-15 and is commonly known as the Great White Throne judgement. This is part of John's final set of seven visions. Notice that the passage starts, 'Then I saw' (v11).

The mention of a great white throne is meant to be impressive. It may be large in size but its greatness is due to the occasion and the one seated on it. 'White' expresses his holiness, and 'throne' that he is the King. These verses are similar in many ways to the vision given to Daniel in Daniel 7:9-10, a court scene where the Ancient of Days takes his seat on a throne and books are opened.

We will examine Revelation 20:11-15 through the usual questions of who, what, why, when and where, starting with 'when', which should be fairly easy to determine. The passage is sandwiched between other events in the series of visions given to John, so, assuming they are chronological to some extent, this is immediately after the end of the Millennium and Satan's final destruction, and immediately before the new heaven and the new earth. This really is the last 'day' of the current age, and what is known as the eternal state is about to begin.

As to where this occurs, the answer seems to be nowhere! The earth and the heavens have fled! The new heaven and new earth are yet to appear. So does this event even have a location? Is it in another non-physical dimension? Yet this occurs after all resurrections have taken place; everyone is now re-embodied. We might be led to conclude that this scene is more symbolic than an actual occasion and that the imagery is more important than locality. We said earlier, we should avoid thinking in terms of an earthly trial or courtroom. It won't be like any judicial court or proceedings we might be used to now. So perhaps the question of 'where' doesn't really apply. But this doesn't make the judgement any the less real. It is the outcome that matters.

Our next consideration is who is the judge, the one seated on the great white throne? If we are ever unfortunate enough to be on trial in an earthly court, the identity of the judge might be important to us. What is he like? In the case of the final Day of Judgement we might ask is it the Father or the Son? Or does it not matter? Some texts say the Father will preside over this judgement (1 Pet. 1:17). Others that he has assigned this role to Jesus (Acts 17:31). In John 5:22 Jesus states, 'The Father judges no one, but has entrusted all judgement to the Son', adding that this is so 'all may honour the Son just as they honour the Father' (v23). Then we read in Romans 14:10 that 'we will all stand before God's judgement seat', while in 2 Corinthians 5:10 it says that 'we must all appear before the judgement seat of Christ'. There is no contradiction in all these statements. Overall, God the Father is our ultimate judge but he has delegated this to Jesus as he died for us. We need not quibble over exactly who is on the judgement throne as there is a complete unity of function in this respect. Their judgements are identical.

We find the same when we look into the book of Revelation. In chapter 4 in general, and more specifically in 19:4 and 21:5, we find it is the Lord God who is seated on the throne. Other verses (5:6, 7:17) mention the Lamb who is standing 'at the centre of the throne', a rather strange phrase but one which indicates the Son's prominent role when it comes to judgement. There is one verse which sums all this up most neatly. In Revelation 22:3 we find the phrase 'The throne of God and of the Lamb'. *The* throne, singular!

As for those who are to be judged, we are told it is 'the dead, great and small' (v12). But there remains considerable debate over exactly who these are. Some say this is everyone who has ever lived; others that it is only those who are to be cast into the lake of fire. But the rest of the passage does not suggest this is the fate of all who are gathered here, just anyone whose name is not written in the book of life (v15). The word 'anyone' implies only some of those there. Likewise with translations that say 'if anyone' or 'and whosoever'. If those before the throne are only unbelievers then verse 15 should read more like, '*as* their names were not written in the book of life they were thrown into the lake of fire'. This would then imply everyone who was there. So attempts to restrict this judgement to unbelievers is unconvincing and not clearly shown in the text. It is better, therefore, to regard the scope of this judgement as a universal gathering of all humanity.

Other phrases back this up. For instance, in verse 13 we have three sources from which the dead were assembled: the sea, death and *hades*. It is difficult to see these as totally distinct from each other. For instance, did those lost at sea not enter death or *hades*? Didn't *hades* contain all the dead anyway? Perhaps this threefold collection is just an expression to indicate all the dead. It covers all bases. No-one can escape this final judgement.

The other phrase used of the dead is 'great and small'. This might simply refer to the fact that human distinctions are irrelevant at this point. It doesn't matter how great or small you were in the eyes of others, all that counts now is how the Judge sees you. But 'great and small' can also be a figure of speech for the whole of humanity. This is an example of what is called a *merism*, a literary device where two contrasting parts of something refer to the whole. For instance, we might say top and bottom to include everything between, or A to Z to mean the whole alphabet.

We may readily understand why unbelievers are judged at this point. After all, this is why they have been raised in the second resurrection (Rev. 20:5). But why believers too? According to Jesus, anyone who believes in him will not be judged, they have already crossed over from death to life (John 5:24).

However, as we have already indicated, believers are still judged according to what we have done but for the purpose of determining our rewards. We will look at this more in the next chapter but, meanwhile, there are some important details in this passage as we consider on what basis the great white throne judgement is made.

The key is the reference to 'books' and 'book'. In verse 12 books are opened. These act as a metaphor for God's knowledge of everything that has happened in each of our lives. These are our personal histories, but there is no mention of them all being read out. It seems God's aim is not to parade before us in great detail everything we have thought and said and done. But it means we know that he knows, and hence we know he can judge accordingly. The writer to the Hebrews warns us that God is fully aware of all the facts. 'Everything is uncovered and laid bare before the eyes of him to whom we must give account' (Heb. 4:13). Never in any human court has all the evidence been as comprehensive as here. This will be the only judgement in all of history that is truly and completely fair.

There is one other book which stands apart from the rest. This is the book of life (v12, also v15). To understand this book and what is in it, we need to realise who owns it. In Revelation 13:8 and 21:27 it is called the Lamb's book of life as it contains the names of those who belong to him, those he acknowledges as his own because they have put their trust in him for salvation. The book of life is found elsewhere in scripture (Ps. 69:28; Dan. 12:1; Phil. 4:3; Rev. 3:5, 17:8). In general it is a register of the righteous. The main point being to keep your name there and avoid it being blotted out. In Revelation, this means remaining faithful to Jesus, following him even unto death.

In Revelation 20:11-15 this book of life contains the names of those who will avoid the lake of fire, hence it is the most important of all the books that will be opened that day. If your name is in the Lamb's book of life at the time of the Great White Throne judgement, then there is nothing to fear. It will be a glorious experience, with an even more glorious future to come. But there is still the matter of the judgement of believers according to the deeds done while living on earth, which we will pick up in our next chapter.

Chapter Nineteen

The Judgement of Believers and the Role of Deeds Done

In the last chapter we looked at an overview of judgement, why it is certain and necessary, and then focused on what is known as the Great White Throne judgement in Revelation 20:11-15. We saw that this is the final judgement of all humanity before the eternal state begins. But scripture also mentions two other judgements. One is in 2 Corinthians 5:10 where Paul talks about the judgement seat of Christ; the other is Jesus' parable in Matthew 25:31-46, sometimes known as the judgement of the nations or that of the sheep and the goats.

The question is whether these are the same event as the Great White Throne judgement, just described slightly differently, or whether they are totally separate. If the latter then when do they occur and what is their purpose? In this chapter we will first attempt to resolve this question, before going on to examine another key issue, the role of works in the judgement of believers. How can we be justified by faith yet on the last day be judged according to works?

We start in 2 Corinthians 5:10 which states, 'For we must all appear before the judgement seat of Christ, so that each of us may receive what is due to us for the things done while in the body, whether good or bad.' This is often known as the *bema* judgement from the Greek word *beimatos* that appears in the verse, usually translated as judgement seat. The word generally refers to a raised platform for public speaking, often in a tribunal. Someone would approach the *bema* to hear the outcome of the administration of justice, including the announcement of rewards as well as punishments. The word also meant the official seat of a judge and often resembled a throne.

The key question regarding 2 Corinthians 5:10 is to whom is Paul referring when he writes 'we must all appear'? This must include the believers in Corinth that he is writing to ('each of us'), and it is unlikely to refer only to Christians there. But does Paul just mean all Christians, or could it be all humankind as in the Great White Throne judgement?

We saw in the last chapter that we shouldn't make a distinction between 'the judgement seat of Christ' in 2 Corinthians 5:10 and 'God's judgement seat' in Romans 14:10, as both Father and Son act as judge with unity of function and purpose. This is made especially clear in Revelation 22:3, where we read about *the* throne of God and of the Lamb. There is a single throne for both as they are jointly making the same judgement. So we cannot conclude on the basis of the words used that the *bema* judgement and the Great White Throne judgement are two separate occasions. If they are different we need to decide this on other grounds.

Meanwhile, we turn to our other passage of interest, Matthew 25:31-46, which is also difficult to interpret in terms of when it occurs and how it fits in with other judgements. One clue is the opening phrase, 'When the Son of Man comes in all his glory'. This verse also makes reference to angels being with him and that he will sit on his glorious throne. The parables which precede this passage concern his return and the need to be ready for it, so it is fair to assume this is at the start of the millennium and not at the end, and hence cannot be another way of describing the Great White Throne judgement, though it does read like that in other ways.

So far there is nothing totally conclusive. It seems we either have three separate judgements occurring at different times, or three slightly differing descriptions of the same one. As we saw in our previous chapter on resurrection, our answer may depend on our view of the Millennium and how it may separate out some of the judgements. At this point, things can get a little complicated!

For Amillennialists and Postmillennialists (see previous chapter for all definitions) there is no need for more than one time of judgement, which must therefore be for everyone at the end of the age when Jesus returns. As Premillennialists believe in two resurrections (believers first, then unbelievers, separated by the Millennium), for them there can, indeed must, be two judgements. Or in some cases more than two, depending on other aspects of this particular belief which we won't go into here!

The first thing that happens after getting our new bodies is to be judged according to what we did in our old body, for rewards and service to come. This will be when the *bema* judgement happens, just before the Millennium starts and we begin to reign with him. Incidentally, for those who believe in an early secret rapture this judgement will probably happen in heaven before any such return.

For some Premillennialists, mainly Dispensationalists, the sheep and goats judgement in Matthew chapter 25 cannot be coincident with the Great White Throne judgement. Instead it occurs on Jesus' return at the start of the Millennium, and this is a judgement of nations (or unbelievers within the various nations or ethnic groups) regarding how they have treated others during the period immediately before his return, known as the tribulation.

The question then is how to identify those Jesus refers to as 'the least of these brothers and sisters of mine' (vv40, 45). Are these just Jews, his brethren after the flesh, or all his eventual followers, Jew and Gentile? He often referred to his disciples as his brothers and sisters so this is a plausible explanation, and by the time of his return there would be many throughout the world, across all the nations.

Another issue with this passage is that it looks like judgement according to works, or at least based upon treating people well. Some have argued that this must be about judging which unbelievers will be allowed to enter the Millennium, a judgement which is based on their actions towards those who belong to Christ. These unbelievers have gained favour from God in this way and so may be allowed to populate the earth during Christ's reign there. This is not an eternal reward, and these 'sheep' are not yet saved but may come to faith during the Millennium if they submit to Christ's reign. The problem with this interpretation is that there is no mention of the Millennium in the passage and the outcomes involve eternal destinies: the sheep inherit the kingdom prepared for them since the creation of the world, and the goats depart into the eternal fire prepared for the devil and his angels. So this particular scenario seems an unlikely explanation of the passage.

Before we leave this passage, we should comment that God does not deal with nations as a whole regarding their eternal destiny. There are unbelievers and believers in every nation, or more precisely every ethnic group. They are gathered as 'all nations', meaning the world, but it is as individual sheep and individual goats that they are separated and judged accordingly for their different destinies.

Given how difficult it is to fit all these judgements together into a satisfactory whole, it is perhaps best to conclude there are two judgements and that these occur at separate times: the *bema* judgement for believers, for rewards at the start of the Millennium; the Great White Throne judgement for everyone at the very end. Believers are at this one also, not for further rewards or a verdict of salvation (this is already determined by their names being in the Lamb's book of life) but as part of the final separation now that the eternal state is about to begin.

This still leaves Matthew chapter 25, which then has to be seen not as another separate event but simply as a parable, hence the animal imagery. This story is intended to provide a general warning of universal judgement to come and an ultimate separation into two different eternal destinies, as well as showing that what we do to others does matter in this regard. As such it contains some of the details found in each of the other two judgements but it is not the same as either. More details on these will follow later through Paul and Jesus himself in the book of Revelation.

Overall, for some, this idea of two judgements separated in time, with an extra story to highlight certain features of both, may not be a totally satisfactory conclusion, and we must admit there is still an element of 'wait and see' about all this. But for now we leave this tricky topic behind and turn to our other main focus in this chapter on judgement, that of God judging believers according to their works.

Scripture consistently testifies that our deeds do count. Our lives will be evaluated on that basis. We read earlier in 2 Corinthians 5:10 that we will receive what is due to us for the things done in the body. Paul also tells the Christians in Rome that God will repay each person according to what they have done (Rom. 2:6, quoting Prov. 24:12 and Ps. 62:12, so this must apply to Old Testament believers also). Then in Revelation 20:13 we have that each person was judged according to what they had done. The same is found in verse 12 where the dead means everyone, not just the wicked.

In other places this is further explained by the idea of rewards. For instance, in Colossians 3:23-24 we are told that 'whatever you do, work at it with all your heart, as working for the Lord, not for human masters, since you know that you will receive an inheritance from the Lord as a reward'. In Matthew 16:27 Jesus said, 'For the Son of Man is going to come in his Father's glory with his angels, and then he will reward each person according to what they have done.' This is backed up in Revelation 11:18 which says, 'The time has come for judging the dead, and for rewarding your servants the prophets', and again in

Revelation 22:12, 'Look, I am coming soon! My reward is with me, and I will give to each person according to what they have done.'

Certain well-known parables emphasise this point, such as those in Matthew 25:14-30 and Luke 19:12-16, as well as that of the sheep and the goats already mentioned later in Matthew chapter 25. Part of the reward is to hear, 'Well done, good and faithful servant! You have been faithful with a few things; I will put you in charge of many things' (Matt. 25:21, 23). In some cases, this is spelled out in specific terms, such as taking charge of cities or sitting on thrones, helping Jesus reign during the Millennium. We may not all get such huge rewards but 1 Corinthians 4:5 assures that when the Lord comes 'each will receive their praise from God', which could be reward enough.

A more detailed discussion is in 1 Corinthians 3:8-15, where the context is the Day (of judgement). All Christians are co-workers with Christ, but not all produce works that endure. God will scrutinise these works and bestow rewards accordingly. Note that it is not the worker but their works that are tested in fire. The fire here is not the lake of fire, but a means of testing the value and permanency of what has been built. Part of the lack of rewards might be shame (not hearing 'well done') or chastisement (as with the man who buried his one talent), or include not serving God more in the Millennium and beyond. No precise details are given, but we should want to avoid such loss.

We also note that these works involve building on the foundation that is Christ, so this doesn't contradict the free gift of salvation by suggesting that these works contribute towards our salvation, but it does indicate an attitude that

Jesus is not just our Saviour but also our Lord and we serve him in return for all that he has done for us.

Moreover, the deeds of true followers of Christ are products of humility: 'we are unworthy servants; we have only done what was our duty' (Luke 17:10). Or even done unaware: 'when did we do all these things?' (Matt. 25:37-39). It is as though such deeds came naturally, without any attempt to earn anything nor any thought of reward! If we do these things in order to gain rewards then no doubt God examines our heart on this and our reward may diminish!

We stress again, on the basis of John 5:24 and elsewhere, that believers have crossed over from death to life, so our deeds are not judged for that purpose. But they are assessed to see how our faith has been lived out. Our faith should be Hebraic, which means not just a creed we recite or something we intellectually assent to, but something we act upon. In Hebraic thinking, faith is more like a verb than a noun. We *do* faith, rather than *have* a faith.

Overall, this is about being faithful in following Christ and what we do to show this. Even something as simple as giving a cup of cold water to one of the least of Christ's disciples brings a reward (Matt. 10:40-42). In general, such works carry great weight as an expression of the outworking of genuine faith. Moreover, our deeds never stand alone. What we do always follows from what we believe. Indeed, it is what we believe which brings our deeds into being at all. Thus they form an excellent basis for judging rewards and the potential for further faithful service.

We are saved by grace through faith alone, but saving faith does not want to stay alone. Faith needs company;

companions for the journey, if you like, for we walk by faith. Faith and deeds are inseparable. They walk hand in hand. If faith remains alone then, according to James, it is dead (Jas 2:14-17). The idea that James and Paul are at odds over faith and works is a false one. Paul often uses the word 'works' to condemn attempts to gain favour with God that way, whereas James refers to them as the natural outcome of faith. Such works complete faith. They make it work. Likewise, Paul talks of justification by faith in terms of legally being declared 'not guilty', whereas when James suggests our works justify us, he means they show evidence of the faith which has made us righteous, not that they in themselves produce righteousness in us.

Knowing that our final judgement is based not on whether we have professed faith but on how we have lived by that faith should guard us against any complacency in the way we live. There is also the reverse point that our faith-based works assure us that our faith is genuine. Paul says we are to examine ourselves to see whether we are in the faith (2 Cor. 13:5). Basically, test yourself by taking a good look at what you are doing. In this way, you can judge yourself first, long before the Day of Judgement arrives.

Does your lifestyle show your faith? Do we aim to please our Lord and Saviour every day knowing that one day we must appear before him to give an account of all we have done? That is the main message of these passages.

As we mentioned in our discussion of resurrection, the writer to the Hebrews lists eternal judgement among the six elementary teachings (Heb. 6:1-2). Whether he means this is easy or just fundamental, he expects us to move on beyond this to other things, which we will do in our remaining chapters when we consider what is called the eternal state, including the new heaven and the new earth, and the alternative which goes under the name of hell.

Chapter Twenty

Hell: A Biblical Overview

Having completed our studies of the intermediate state with the topics of resurrection and judgement, we are now ready to enter what is known as the eternal state, which means we must tackle the horrific idea of hell, also known as the lake of fire.

The subject of hell is such an unpleasant one that many wish it wasn't in the Bible at all. For instance, in his book *The Problem of Pain*, C.S. Lewis declares there is no other doctrine he would more willingly remove from Christianity, yet at the same time he accepts that it has the full support of scripture and especially of the teaching of Jesus himself. Indeed, it is Jesus who tells us more about hell than anyone else, so it has to be taken seriously. And therein lies our dilemma. The doctrine of hell may be the most offensive and disturbing of them all, yet removing it requires us to ignore Jesus or regard him as a false teacher in this respect. And if Jesus was wrong about hell, how can we trust what he says about heaven?

Nevertheless, the topic of hell is often now disbelieved, or at least ignored by most Christians who seem embarrassed to discuss it or prefer to assume that somehow it is not relevant today. As such, hell has become a disappearing doctrine. There is a determination to reject its main ideas or blot it out completely from our thinking. And this is understandable. If scripture was not so clear and conclusive, who would want to believe it? But we cannot disregard something in the Bible just because we don't like it. So we must tackle this, albeit with care and sensitivity. Part of which is to recognise that many ideas we might have about hell don't actually come from the Bible. There have been additions and embellishments over the centuries. We need to assess how valid these are.

We start with the traditional definition of hell and some possible objections to it. In biblical terms, the punishment associated with hell is that of everlasting conscious torment. While some aspects of the nature of hell may be debatable, the three elements that always stand out are eternal, conscious and torment.

Some of the main objections to this are obvious. Can an everlasting afterlife of perpetual torture be justified? This is a moral objection based upon our sense of fairness which makes us question whether such punishment really fits the crime. Surely endless torment is too excessive whatever sins have been committed? This seems like the equivalent of capital punishment for a parking offence. Even if some kind of punishment is necessary for those who don't repent and find salvation, should it be this severe? We may accept punishments that reform or deter others but this seems purely to be about retribution.

And then there is the matter of God's love. Can everlasting torment be consistent with this? We may wonder whether God himself can endure doing this to some of his creatures. What are his feelings in this matter? How does he cope? Does he have conflicting emotions?

It could also be argued that the existence of hell suggests God has somehow failed. It doesn't speak well of him or bring him glory. He could, indeed should, have done better.

Moreover, it is often said that the doctrine of hell drives many away from accepting Christianity at all. Some of the more fervent atheists, such as Bertrand Russell, have stated that Jesus' teaching on hell is a serious flaw in his moral character and hence he is not worthy to be followed at all. In particular, they argue, who would want to be in heaven with a God who sends people to hell?

It is not difficult to understand how such objections have led to various alternatives to the traditional view of hell being proposed or at least to certain adjustments being made, including by sincere Christians who want to lessen the impact of this doctrine and allow for a more friendly approach to evangelism. We shall examine some of the alternatives later in the next chapter. Meanwhile, let's begin to survey what the Bible actually teaches on this matter.

We have stated earlier in this book that there isn't an exact word in the Hebrew scriptures for hell, nor indeed a clear concept of it. We saw that *sheol* in the Old Testament is not to be equated with hell. This is simply the realm of the dead which may be an undesirable place of no return but without any particular idea of punishment taking place.

Some earthly judgements in the Old Testament (for instance, that of Sodom and Gomorrah) do seem to foreshadow later aspects of hell, but hell as such does not feature in the Hebrew scriptures. At most there is a slight hint of this, but with little clarity. For instance, in Daniel 12:1-3 we read of two distinct fates: everlasting life and everlasting contempt. This distinction comes into sharper focus in the intertestamental period with the concept of a division within *sheol* between the righteous and the wicked, something which Jesus picks up concerning *hades* (the Greek equivalent of *sheol*) in his parable of the rich man and Lazarus in Luke chapter 16 which we have looked at previously.

In effect, it is not until we reach the New Testament that we find a fiery torturous afterlife for the wicked. Here, for the first time in the biblical literature, we see what we now normally think of as hell. Even then this occurs only in certain parts of the New Testament, most notably in the gospels of Matthew, Mark and Luke, and the book of Revelation where the graphic picture of the horrors to come is summed up through the phrase 'the lake of fire' or 'the fiery lake of burning sulphur' (Rev. 19:20, 20:10-15, 21:8). The only other use of the word 'hell' is in James 3:6, a verse about the damage the misuse of language can cause. Here the imagery of fire is used to describe how the tongue can be an instrument of such harm. It can set the whole course of one's life on fire and itself be 'set on fire by hell'.

As we mentioned earlier, just about everything we learn about hell comes from the mouth of Jesus. Why is this? Perhaps God reasoned that if we heard about hell from the most truthful and loving person who ever walked on the earth we would be more likely to accept it and take it more seriously. Hearing about hell from Jesus makes the warnings more real and terrible, and also makes the teaching harder to reject or reassess than if it came from, for instance, an Old Testament prophet such as Jeremiah, or the apostle Paul.

So how exactly did Jesus describe hell? Part of the answer lies in his choice of a specific Hebrew word, *gehenna*. This is the word we translate into English as 'hell'. In addition to the isolated case in James 3:6, this word occurs 11 times across the synoptic gospels, mainly in Matthew: see Matthew 5:22, 29, 30 (parallels in Mark 9:43-48), Matthew 10:28 (cf Luke 12:5), Matthew 18:9, 23:15, 33.

Other verses indicate the features of this hellish existence, such as outer darkness, a blazing unquenchable fire, worms which never die, and weeping and gnashing of teeth (Matt. 8:12, 13:42, 49-50, 22:13, 24:51, 25:30, 41, 46; Luke 13:28). Incidentally, the phrase 'gnashing of teeth' refers not to agony but to anger and opposition, as in Acts 7:54, and the idea of worms that do not die and fire that cannot be quenched occurs previously in the Old Testament (see Isa. 66:24).

Jesus most likely chose the word *gehenna* as it was already known to the Jews of his day as an actual place with a specific history. *Gehenna* means the Valley of Hinnom. It is first mentioned in Joshua 15:8, 18:16 regarding the allocation of land for the tribes of Judah and Benjamin. But more significantly it became infamous as a site for child sacrifice. During the time of kings Ahaz and Manasseh, children were burnt alive there as an offering to Canaanite gods, especially Molech (see 2 Kgs 16:3, 21:6; 2 Chron. 28:1-3, 33:6). Clearly this was offensive to God and forbidden by him (Lev. 18:21; Deut. 12:31). Thus the Valley of Hinnom became known as a place of hostility and opposition to God. Part of this valley was also called Topheth, meaning abomination or desolation. We first come across this designation in 2 Kings 23:10 when the reforming king Josiah took steps to end such atrocities. He 'desecrated' Topheth, in that he tore down the altars used in child sacrifice making the place unusable for further practices of this kind. Yet its history remained, as did its association with extreme evil.

Jeremiah also makes mention of Topheth in the Valley of Hinnom, declaring that it will be renamed the Valley of Slaughter as there God will destroy all idolaters, leaving their corpses to be consumed by scavengers (Jer. 7:30-33, also 19:5-6, 32:35). As the Jews of Jesus' day already understood *gehenna* in such terms, it is easy to see why he took this up as an appropriate and graphic illustration of the final place of punishment of the wicked, extending it from the idolaters of earlier times to all those who ultimately reject God and his ways.

This valley, which is just outside Jerusalem on its southern edge, is so deep that sunlight never reaches part of it, so it is fitting to describe it as a place of outer darkness. It is also often said that after the time of Josiah the valley became the rubbish tip for the city of Jerusalem, a place into which residents threw their garbage, thus creating the association with worms and continual fire. However, some scholars now dispute this. They say there is no evidence that the valley was ever used in this way in biblical times.

It is simply a popular myth without any support, either from archaeology or the Bible or any other writings or teaching of the time. The earliest such mention may be by the rabbinical teacher David Kimhi, who wrote in Europe in the early thirteenth century. In his commentary on Psalm 27, he describes the valley as a repugnant place into which filth and corpses are thrown. This may well be referring to the practice in Roman times of how the corpses of those who had been crucified were disposed of. This may well have been the fate of Jesus' body if Joseph of Arimathea had not offered his tomb. It is also thought that this valley is the site of Judas' suicide, adding a further connection with death and destruction.

It is also interesting to note that the derivation of the English word 'hell' is of 'a hidden dark place'. Some suggest it relates to a tailor's 'hell', the name given to a basket or similar container hidden under his bench where he threw all the unwanted scraps of material which were no longer useful, another similar image of waste disposal.

But whatever we may decide about this aspect of *gehenna*, we can say for certain that the Hinnom valley is not used as a rubbish dump today. Moreover, although the nature and purpose of a municipal dumping ground might offer some clue towards what Jesus was trying to convey, to reduce the image of hell merely to that of a rubbish tip is to severely lessen its impact. Jesus had something much more sinister in mind. The Valley of Hinnom had come to represent total rebellion against God. It was a place associated with the worship of false gods, spiritual darkness and barbaric cruelty. As such it epitomised the total rejection of the Lord by men, and was thus a fitting way to describe the ultimate rejection of men by God. The fate of those who rebelled against God in favour of other gods was to be cast away and shut out from his presence, as echoed by Jesus' own words 'depart from me' (see, for instance, Matt. 25:41).

We end this chapter on the topic of hell by looking at some other words used in scripture to describe the underworld, or part of it.

In his second letter, Peter refers to *tartarus* (2 Pet. 2:4), a word which appears nowhere else in scripture. In fact, he uses a verbal form of the word which means 'to cast into Tartarus', and so translations often use the phrase 'sent them to hell'. But what did Peter mean by using this word, and who exactly are sent there?

In classical literature Tartarus was a mythological subterranean realm where divine punishment was meted out on those who were particularly wicked, including disobedient gods as well as rebellious humans. It was considered to be the opposite of Elysium, also known as the Elysian Fields, a place of eternal bliss where the righteous would receive their reward.

Jewish writers between the Old and New Testaments also employed the word *tartarus*, in their case as a place of confinement for wicked angels. So in his letter Peter is using a term that is familiar to his readers, whether of Greek or Jewish background. Moreover, we see in this verse that he also refers to angels who have sinned, in particular a special category of fallen angels. These are also mentioned in Jude verse 6. It is usually assumed these are the angels (or 'sons of God') we find in Genesis chapter 6 who were instrumental in increasing wickedness on the earth before the flood, including bringing about the Nephilim. This is a tricky passage to interpret and much disputed, but whoever these rebellious angels were and whatever they had done, they have now been *tartarised*, locked away as in a dungeon, and they will remain there until the final judgement so they cannot cause any more damage on earth or wreak further havoc. We may not fully understand what Peter is saying in this part of his letter but one thing we can be sure of is that *tartarus* does not have anything to do with the fate or punishment of humans, only angels.

Another word with similar connotations is the 'abyss' (Greek, *abusso*). This word features many times in the book of Revelation (Rev. 9:1-2, 11; 11:7; 17:8; 20:1, 3). But the first mention of this idea is in Genesis 1:2 where the Hebrew equivalent, *tehom*, usually translated as 'deep', refers to the depths of the earth or, more usually, the ocean depths. Today scientists refer to those parts of our oceans which lie between 4km and 6km below the surface as the abyssal zones. Even further below these are the hadal zones which can range as far down as 11km, one example being the Mariana Trench, the deepest part of the Pacific Ocean. Above these two zones lie the twilight zone, just below the surface, and then the midnight zone. Here light has already disappeared, leaving a world of absolute blackness that stretches for miles further down into the abyssal and hadal zones.

But biblically the Abyss represents far more than just a deep mass of water. There are spiritual connotations too, with connections to the grave, to chaos and to darkness. Demons knew this was the worst of all possible places for them to be sent. When Jesus cast out the demons known as Legion, they begged him repeatedly not to order them to go in to the Abyss (Luke 8:30-31). The Abyss represented extreme imprisonment, a place of total exclusion and separation. It will be where Satan will be chained up for 1,000 years (Rev. 20:1-3). But, like *tartarus*, the Abyss is not intended for humans, and so need not concern us further.

Finally, we should mention the word 'inferno' which comes from the Latin *infernum*. This Latin word was originally the equivalent of *hades*, the abode of the dead, but later became associated with the place of the damned and so in English is often regarded as another word for 'hell'. Many will have heard of this word through Dante's Inferno, which is the title of the first part of his epic poem *The Divine Comedy*, written in the fourteenth century. Here, Dante imagines a journey through the realms of the afterlife, including the so-called nine circles of hell. As this has no real biblical basis, we will leave it there.

Meanwhile, in our next chapter we will consider various modern alternatives to the biblical view of hell, as well as correct many of the myths and misconceptions that often affect the way people think of hell.

Chapter Twenty-One

Hell: Modern Alternatives

Our last chapter focused on the biblical definition of hell as eternal conscious torment, looking in particular at Jesus' use of the word *gehenna*. Now we explore this topic further, picking up on how objections to the biblical view of hell have led to recent redefinitions and reinterpretations.

Arguments against the existence of a biblical hell do not just come from those outside Christian circles. Many Christians today also question this. Even evangelicals, who uphold scripture and therefore the reality of hell in some form, still disagree over what it is really like. So overall it is not unexpected that in recent times alternatives to the biblical description of hell have been proposed. But what exactly are these new ideas and how should they be evaluated?

For many, hell is just a metaphor for how terrible life can be here and now. It refers to the bad experiences we suffer in this life, either through our own making or the actions of others. The French atheist and existentialist writer Jean-Paul Sartre once famously wrote, 'Hell is other people', implying hell is best seen as the conflict and torment we bring upon each other. In short, we make life hell for others.

Such views aim to lessen the impact of hell by bringing it forward into life before death, thus removing from it anything to do with God or eternal punishment. Generally, ways of reducing hell to something more palatable involve saying it is only temporary in duration or merely remedial in purpose; either hell doesn't last forever or its intention is corrective not punitive. We will look at the two main versions of this, known as universalism and annihilationism.

Universalism, or universal salvation, teaches that everyone gets to heaven eventually. Christ died for all without exception, so God will ensure this sacrifice is effective for all, otherwise he will have failed in his purpose or shown himself to be too weak to achieve what he wants, which is to reconcile all things to himself. So by readjusting our idea of hell in this way we are helping God out by protecting him from such accusations, especially that he is unjust or cruel.

The idea of universalism first emerged among the Greek-thinking church fathers we discussed in an earlier chapter, such as Clement and Origen. At several points in his treatise called *On First Principles*, Origen describes hell not as a place of eternal damnation but more as a divine correctional facility, a sort of rehabilitation programme. This is how God will bring about the restoration of all things. Even Satan will be saved and find a place in heaven, though only after some very severe punishment! Thus hell is redefined, even redesigned. It is no longer to be regarded as Christians have historically believed. Instead any punishment is temporary. All will escape at some point.

Those who support universalism point to the word 'all' in texts such as 1 Corinthians 15:22 ('as in Adam all die, so in Christ all will be made alive') and Romans 5:18 which explains that just as Adam's sin brought condemnation to us all, so Christ's death 'resulted in justification and life for all people'. However, the word 'all' does not always mean absolutely everyone. It can have certain limitations depending on context, simply referring to everyone within a certain category. So 1 Corinthians 15:22 can mean 'all those who are in Christ will be made alive', not the entire human race, which would contradict other scriptures and the gospel message itself. Evangelism would no longer be about persuading people to accept Christ and avoid hell. Instead it would just involve telling them they are already saved and can look forward to heaven, even if there might be a bit of corrective punishment first.

For these reasons, and others, it is clear why few Christian teachers support universalism. But they would still prefer hell to be something less than a place of eternal torment, so the tendency is to favour the other main option, annihilationism.

While annihilationism does not teach that everyone will eventually get to heaven, it does assert that no-one will be in hell forever. The wicked will suffer conscious torment but only for a while. After that, God will annihilate them completely so that they no longer exist. Thus hell is redefined as terminal rather than eternal. It involves a finite period of punishment though with everlasting effects in that, sooner or later, those sent there are fully consumed by the fires of hell and cease to exist at all. This view has several advantages. Firstly, the punishment seems more proportionate, especially if the length of time before annihilation is based upon the severity of wickedness in this life. It is therefore easier to justify in moral terms and to defend God against the charge of being unjust and cruel. In addition, once all its human inhabitants have been sent into oblivion, hell can still remain forever as a place of eternal punishment for the devil and his angels, something which no-one has ever seemed to object to.

Annihilationism suggests humans can cease to exist, but is this so? Weren't we all created immortal? The argument made here is that humanity is *not* inherently immortal. Instead we have what is called 'conditional immortality'. Only God is truly immortal, though he created us with the potential for immortality by being in relationship with him. At the Fall, we lost all that. Sin cut us off from God and so we were no longer guaranteed immortality. But once redeemed by Christ, immortality is granted to us as part of our salvation via our new resurrection bodies. Immortality for humans is thus conditional upon accepting the salvation offered through Christ. Those who don't accept salvation do not, therefore, have immortal life and so at death or sometime later can cease to exist. Is this a biblical position? In 1 Corinthians 15:53-54, Paul talks about the mortal being clothed with immortality, implying the new resurrection bodies of believers will take on an immortality they do not currently have. But nothing is said here about the nature of the resurrected bodies of unbelievers, whether they are also immortal and hence indestructible. This is a matter scholars still debate and so the 'conditional immortality' aspect of the annihilation idea remains uncertain.

Proponents of annihilationism point to biblical texts which refer to the *destruction* of the wicked which, they argue, implies they are destroyed completely and so cease to exist. For example, in Matthew 10:28 we read that we are to fear the one who can destroy (*apolesai*) both body and soul in hell. Further variations of the Greek word *apollumi* occur elsewhere. In Philippians 3:19 the destiny of the enemies of the cross of Christ is one of 'destruction' (*apoleya*), and 2 Peter 3:7 announces the 'destruction [*apoleias*] of the ungodly'. But in none of these cases does the word mean to pass out of existence. In fact, nowhere in the New Testament does *apollumi* mean annihilation or extinction. Rather it refers to the destructive effect upon someone or their ruin, a loss not of *being* but of *well-being*. Another example is when perfume was poured out on Jesus' head. Some said it had been 'wasted' or destroyed, not in the sense that it no longer existed but that it could have no further use or be sold (Mark 14:4). This idea applies to those in hell. They are now wasted and cannot be reused. Unredeemed and now irredeemable, still alive but with no further purpose. Perished and perishing, like an elastic band that has lost its elasticity. It cannot be used any more. It is only fit to be discarded.

A different Greek word for destruction occurs in other texts. 1 Thessalonians 5:3 says that destruction (*olethros*) will come upon people suddenly, and 2 Thessalonians 1:9 states that those who do not obey the gospel will be punished with everlasting destruction (*olethron*), but again this word implies no sense of complete extinction. In fact, the latter verse contains the word 'everlasting' and we turn to this now.

Many places in the New Testament refer to hell as being eternal or everlasting, whether in terms of worms that do not die and fire that is not quenched (Mark 9:48) or just as eternal punishment (Matt. 25:46) or the punishment of eternal fire (Jude 7). But this aspect of hell still remains a main point of dispute. Can it really be 'for ever and ever'?

The key verse in this respect is Matthew 25:46 which refers both to eternal punishment (*kolasin aionion*) and eternal life (*zoein aionion*) with the same word for 'eternal' in each case. We would certainly hope that eternal life means for ever, so we must assume the same for those whose fate is eternal punishment.

The book of Revelation regularly uses the expression 'for ever and ever' and we would expect a consistency over the duration intended. The phrase is used for the worship of God (1:6, 4:9, 5:13), the life of God himself (4:10, 10:6) and the reign of the saints (22:5). All these must surely be unending so we must expect the same when we see the phrase occurring elsewhere, including the torment of the lake of fire (14:11, 19:3, 20:10). In fact, Revelation uses a most emphatic form in Greek, *eis tous aionas ton aionon*, which can be translated as 'unto the ages of the ages'. The strength of this expression is created by taking the word for the greatest length of time (*aeon*), pluralising it, then multiplying it by its own plural and adding definite articles (the). This could hardly be stressed more forcefully, though on two occasions the extra phrase 'day and night' is added to provide further emphasis to the ceaselessness of what is being described.

Overall, it is clear that in the Bible eternal means without end. There is no hint anywhere that the wicked suffer only for a finite period. There is no respite, no slipping away into peaceful non-existence.

So if alternatives such as annihilation and universalism cannot be sustained from the biblical texts, then we must accept that the traditional definition of eternal conscious torment is accurate. However, we should apply clear thinking to what is intended by this, and avoid any myths and misconceptions, as well as the excesses of medieval literature and art. So we finish this chapter by trying to gain a better understanding of this important but difficult biblical topic.

Firstly, we must realise that the nature of hell is often graphically depicted for effect, and this is made more powerful through the use of symbolic and figurative language. Images such as undying worms, unquenchable fire, extreme darkness and a lake of burning sulphur are chosen to convey the horrifying state of hell. In some cases these seem contradictory, for instance fire and darkness, as flames give off light as well as heat. These are both powerful figures but for them to coexist means they have to be metaphors. Also, literal fire usually consumes whatever is placed within it, which would deny the eternal nature of hell. However, we can't dismiss symbols as though they have no real meaning. We have to think through what they signify. For instance, being burned by fire is one of the most excruciating pains we know, so the imagery is appropriate. But we must realise that even if not every description of hell is to be taken literally (whoever heard of worms that never die?), then hell is still a literal place, just with a reality beyond normal speech. God often teaches us through symbols and images. In this case the awfulness of hell requires figurative language, carefully chosen to typify the horrors.

There are several misconceptions made about hell that need to be corrected. One is that repentance occurs in hell. The weeping and gnashing of teeth are not about sorrow or repentance but rage. This is an act of defiance based upon anger and enmity (see Job 16:9; Ps. 35:16 Ps. 37:12; Acts 7:54). Hell does not consist of souls in remorse. This is a place of ongoing rebellion against God's rule.

Another misconception is that the devil is in charge of hell and its sufferings, having fun at our expense. Despite what art and literature often depict, humans are not sent there to be punished by the devil and his demons. The devil is not our tormentor; rather, he is *being* tormented, perhaps even more so than humans. The primary purpose of hell is as a place specifically prepared for the devil and his angels (Matt. 25:41), for their suffering and ultimate destruction (Rev. 20:10). If humans are there too, it is not for the devil's pleasure!

It is also usually assumed that everyone in hell suffers equally. But is this really the case? Might there be varying degrees of punishment? There are hints of this in some of the things Jesus says. He talks about disobedient servants receiving differing amounts of blows (Luke 12:47-48), some cities finding the Day of Judgement 'more bearable' than others (Matt. 10:15, 11:22), and some teachers of the law being punished 'most severely' (Luke 20:47). Also, in Romans 2:6 Paul reminds us God will repay each person according to what they have done. Does this just apply to rewards for believers or might it also include the punishment of the wicked? The principles of justice suggest there ought to be greater and lesser punishments, but isn't hell already as bad as it can possibly be? How can it be worse for some? Some argue here that because this is *conscious* torment then suffering can vary in intensity and effect, but to suggest anything more on how this might apply is to speculate beyond what the Bible offers.

Perhaps the worst misconception about hell is to regard it as a sort of divine torture chamber, a place where God enjoys tormenting those who have rejected him. Yet we never seem to ask how God himself feels about hell and the need for it. What is it really like from his perspective? If hell is necessary because divine justice requires it, then what else is God to do? Moreover, to suggest it is God who is torturing people in hell is absurd because he is not there to do so! In fact, hell is often defined in terms of the absence of God. It is a totally God*less* place. Which is why being there is an existence devoid of anything good. There can be no joy, peace, hope or love in hell, because God is the source of all these things and he is not there to provide them. Thus separation from God is a severe punishment in itself. This is what the Bible calls the second death (Rev. 20:6), a complete and irrevocable separation from God and everything good that comes from him. In the end, God gives up the sinner to the consequences of his unbelief and rejection of God's goodness.

We should also stress that no-one is in hell yet. This is a place for re-embodied people. Being consigned to hell comes after their resurrection and judgement, as part of the eternal state. However, from Jesus' story in Luke chapter 16, it does seem that suffering occurs for the wicked during the intermediate state, while in *hades*. At this point, while believers go to be with the Lord, the wicked are already separated from God and so begin to experience what hell will be like.

Hell is more than punishment *for* sin; it is the logical outcome *of* sin, in particular unrepentant sin which in itself is an act of rebellion and defiance. The enormity of such sin is beyond our comprehension. Its seriousness must be seen in terms of the one we sin against, God himself, the only one who is perfectly holy. In the end the extent of our sin can only be measured by God, and so only he can determine the extent of any punishment that is deserved.

To talk of hell may seem offensive to modern ears but we should always bear in mind how offensive our rebellion is to God. His own children have rejected him and his ways. To live apart from God in this life is a matter of some seriousness and severity, so to do so forever must be even more so.

We must stress that God does not choose hell for people or people for hell. Ultimately, they choose it for themselves by spurning God and all he has done for them. Thus it can rightly be said that the pain of absolute abandonment is of their own making.

Moreover, God does not hate sinners or desire to punish them. Rather, his desire is that humans do not end up in the same place as the devil and his angels. For that reason, he has provided a way of salvation to avoid this. Jesus died on the cross to ensure that hell need not become our destiny. But accepting that offer of salvation is a matter of free will. God created us with free will and so it must play out in all matters of life and death and what comes after.

It has been necessary to spend quite some time on this difficult topic, but we can move on in our next chapter and focus on something much more pleasant – heaven.

Chapter Twenty-Two

Heaven:
A Biblical Overview

Mention heaven and what comes to mind for most people? Usually pictures of clouds and angels, harps and halos, pearly gates and streets of gold. But how much of this is biblical? And aren't these mainly symbols anyway? Is there any kind of reality behind all this?

A further issue is how attractive all this is, even to Christians let alone others. Do we look forward to heaven with joy and hope? Does an eternity like this excite us? And is this the best we can offer those seeking to understand the Christian faith before committing to it? It shouldn't surprise us if they think our view of heaven is something akin to a fairy tale, the result of an over eager imagination. Pie in the sky when we die! At best, it may seem like a harmless delusion. Even if heaven doesn't exist it's good to have something to look forward to as compensation for a distressing and painful life now. For others, the Christian view of heaven comes across as a dangerous distraction from this life now. 'Imagine there's no heaven', they might sing. It would be a better world now if we all took that attitude.

For some, heaven is whatever we want it to be. We make our own heaven. We have seen previously how some today think of hell purely in terms of bad experiences in this life. Likewise we talk about heaven in terms of 'heaven on earth' or say 'this is heaven' when we experience something most pleasurable here and now. If there is anything afterwards it will surely be a continuation of what makes us happy now. For others, heaven may be the place where everyone (or nearly everyone) goes after death, or that it is simply where God lives. It is his address. After all, he must live somewhere. It may not be thought of these days as 'beyond the clouds' but there must be some kind of realm, perhaps beyond time and space, inhabited by God and his angels. Maybe we'll go and join them when we die?

We may well wonder how so many ideas and such varied opinions have become commonplace. Furthermore, if heaven is so essential to the Christian faith, why has it been allowed to be so misunderstood? And how can we correct such misconceptions? The answer as always is to look at scripture, so let's start our survey of what the Bible says about heaven by looking at the words used.

The Hebrew word is *shamayim*, the Greek equivalent being *ouranos*. Both are plural words and so are often translated as 'heavens'. They are also flexible words with three meanings. The first is the sky or atmosphere, where birds fly, clouds gather and from which rain falls. The second is outer space, the location of celestial bodies, such as the planets and the stars. This is what God 'stretches out' in Psalm 104:2. The third is what we usually regard as the 'dwelling place of God', also called the heavenly realm.

These three types of 'heaven' can be summed up as meteorological, astronomical and theological.

Of the 420 times that *shamayim* is used in the Old Testament, about 75 per cent refer to either the sky or the solar system, the other 25 per cent to the heavenly realm. In the New Testament, *ouranos* has the same three meanings but now it is mostly referring to God's dwelling place.

Some English translations use 'heavens' (plural) for the sky or outer space but 'heaven' (singular) for where God lives. Here the original word is still plural but is translated as singular as a way of providing clarity that we are definitely referring to the dwelling place of God. Another way of doing this is through the phrase 'the heavenly realms' which maintains the plural. We find this several times in Ephesians. For instance, we have been blessed in the heavenly realms with every spiritual blessing in Christ (1:3); Christ is seated at God's right hand in the heavenly realms (1:20); God has seated us with Christ in the heavenly realms (2:6). Some versions may use the phrase 'heavenly *places*', with the second word in italics to indicate it is absent in the Greek but has been added to help tidy up the English translation and avoid using the more awkward 'in the heavenlies'.

Another phrase for the dwelling place of God is 'the third heaven'. Paul used this in 2 Corinthians 12:2 when describing his experience of being 'caught up to the third heaven'. It seems Paul is happy to talk in terms of how the universe was understood in his times. The earth was regarded as flat with several layers of heaven above it. Some Jewish traditions taught there were seven levels, stretching upwards to the highest of them all, the seventh heaven, a phrase we still find in use today. But this rabbinic model of heaven is only a tradition. As we have seen, the Bible thinks not in terms of seven but three: sky, outer space, God's dwelling place, and it is this 'triple decker' approach which allows Paul to talk of the third heaven.

This idea of the 'third heaven' seems to be equivalent to a similar term found in the Old Testament, namely 'the highest heavens'. In Deuteronomy 10:14 we read, 'To the LORD your God belong the heavens, even the highest heavens . . .' Then in 1 Kings 8:27 there is: 'The heavens, even the highest heaven, cannot contain you.' Literally, this phrase is 'the heaven of heavens', a typical Hebraic way of describing a superlative, similar to the Holy of Holies meaning the holiest place of all. So we could talk of God inhabiting the heavenliest heaven, or the most heavenly of all heavens! But perhaps the highest heaven will suffice!

We have been referring to heaven as God's dwelling place, and rightly so, for there are many scriptural references to back this up (see for instance, Deut. 26:15; 1 Kgs 8:30, 39, 43, 49; 2 Chron. 30:27). But heaven is much more than just an address for where God lives. Heaven is best thought of not just as where God dwells but as the place from which he rules. Heaven is his throne room. In fact, in Isaiah 66:1 the Lord says, 'Heaven is my throne', not just where his throne is situated. Jesus agrees when he says we are not to swear by heaven, 'for it is God's throne' (Matt. 5:34). So to say God dwells in heaven is actually to proclaim that he reigns over all his creation.

We can also say heaven is where God's presence is fully known and his will perfectly done, which is why we pray to our Father in heaven and ask that his will be done on earth *'as it is in heaven'* (Matt. 6:10). Heaven can therefore be regarded as the seat of God's power, the control room for all creation. It is here that decisions are made and commands are issued. It was from the throne of heaven that God spoke creation into being. It is also where his holiness and majesty are displayed in their fullness, and it is in heaven that he is worshipped unreservedly.

A question often asked is, 'What is heaven really like?' But this is not a particularly helpful question. In many ways heaven is indescribable. We rely upon visions and symbolism to get any kind of picture but these will always remain inadequate and somewhat difficult to grasp. So when trying to understand heaven it is perhaps more beneficial to focus on what goes on there, rather than a detailed description of its appearance. We often refer to this as looking at function rather than form. In particular, our emphasis should be more upon the God of heaven than heaven itself. What does he do there? What does he say? What happens in his presence? These are perhaps more meaningful questions than what heaven is like as a place.

Another common question is, 'Where is heaven?' This can also be unhelpful and misleading. We have been using the words 'place' and 'it is where . . .', as though heaven has a particular location. This is perhaps a natural thing to do, but terminology like this suggests something territorial, a region set apart for a special purpose. This can give a false impression, especially nowadays as the idea of a layered cosmology is no longer recognised. Today we readily accept that heaven is not to be found in the sky, or even beyond it in outer space. So we have to think differently. Similarly with hell, which can no longer be regarded as being 'under' the earth or deep within it.

To get any idea of 'where' heaven is we must start by realising that it is completely outside of our normal physical existence. It does not lie within the space-time dimensions in which we live. Indeed we might say heaven is not so much *in* a different dimension of reality, but that it *is* a different dimension of reality. It is therefore generally beyond our current senses, hidden from sight unless God specifically reveals something, as he did to John in the book of Revelation and also when Elisha asked God to open his servant's eyes (2 Kgs 6:17). Heaven is therefore a dimension of creation beyond the one we currently inhabit. This isn't less real, but more real, or at least one day it will be more real than anything we can currently experience.

So we can say that heaven is all around us, very close but not usually apparent, which would explain how the resurrected Jesus could repeatedly appear and disappear, and how he could still be thought of as being with his disciples even when he was not with them in any discernible way. When he ascended to heaven, the disciples might have thought of him as then being a long way away. In one sense that was true, but his permanent heavenly existence did not mean that he was completely out of range.

Another point here is that we saw earlier how scripture defines heaven as the throne of God. The important thing about a throne is not what it looks like or where it is, but what it represents: power, authority, someone ruling over a kingdom. Our King may have his throne in Buckingham Palace, and perhaps several others elsewhere, but in effect he takes his 'throne' with him wherever he goes. It is not restricted to one place. In these terms, the whereabouts of heaven takes on a new meaning. Wherever God is, there is heaven.

Having said all that, the language of locality may still be used to good effect to make a particular point about heaven without being related to location at all. For instance, in talking to his disciples Jesus mentions his Father's house which has many rooms and that he is going there to prepare a place for them (John 14:2). A place by definition is something physical, but it can also be used as a figure of speech. Here Jesus wants his followers to feel that heaven will be like a large family home, or a big community, but one that is prepared in advance with each individual in mind. In fact, some translations talk of the Father's mansion (*oikia*) containing many homes (*monai*).

But if you do refer to heaven as a place, another question naturally follows. How, then, do I get there? The conversation between Jesus and his disciples in John 14:4-6 continued along these lines:

Jesus: You know the way to the place I am going.

Thomas: Lord, we don't know where you are going,
so how can we know the way?

Jesus: I am the way.

The point here is that the way to heaven is Jesus himself. You want to get to heaven? Then you have to let Jesus take you. There is no other way. There is no separate road map, no X marks the spot for you to discover on your own. But follow him and you'll find yourself there.

This is similar to how Jesus spoke to one of the criminals being crucified next to him when he said, 'Today you will be *with me* in paradise' (Luke 23:43, italics mine). Again, Jesus related a heavenly afterlife directly to himself, to being where he was or soon would be. Being in paradise and being with Jesus were equivalent. So you needn't worry about where it is or how to get there.

But what did Jesus mean by 'paradise'? Here is another biblical word often associated with heaven. As well as Luke 23:43, the Greek word, *paradeiso*, occurs twice more in the New Testament (2 Cor. 12:4; Rev. 2:7). So how did this word come about and what does it mean?

The word 'paradise' originates from a Persian root and describes a large walled garden or park. For instance, the Greek version of this word is used in the Septuagint, the Greek translation of the Old Testament, to refer to the Garden of Eden (Gen. 2:8; Ezek. 28:13). As such, it represents a place of peace and harmony and also of God's presence, somewhere he feels at home when visiting earth. The Jews believed that God would one day restore Eden on earth, and so paradise was the word they began to use to describe a place for righteous souls after death. Here is another portrayal of heaven based upon a physical locality. If you imagine a royal estate that surrounds or is adjacent to a palatial residence, such as Sandringham or Windsor Great Park, then you will get the picture.

There are many times in the New Testament where both Jesus and heaven are mentioned. Jesus describes how he came down to earth from the heavenly places (John 3:13, 6:38). It is also where he returned immediately after his resurrection, in his new body (John 20:17). According to

Hebrews 9:24, 'He entered heaven itself, now to appear before us in God's presence.' Heaven is where Jesus is now (Eph. 6:9; Col. 4:1), seated and reigning (Eph. 2:6), with angels, authorities and powers in submission to him (1 Pet. 3:22). It is also from heaven that one day he will return to earth (Acts 1:11).

Jesus is now in heaven, though he remains 'the man Christ Jesus' (1 Tim. 2:5). He is a heavenly being, but not in the same way as before his incarnation. He is now a heavenly man, one whose image we will one day bear (1 Cor. 15:49). Moreover, Jesus can still appear on earth without ever leaving heaven. When on Patmos the apostle John saw a heavenly figure (Rev. 1:12-20) and while there is no mention of any name, John had no doubt it was Jesus. As we said earlier about God generally, wherever Jesus goes from now on, heaven goes with him.

Other verses remind us that heaven is a place for departed saints (Phil. 1:23; Rev. 20:4), it is where our citizenship now lies (Phil. 3:20) and where God keeps our future inheritance, our salvation to come (1 Pet. 1:4). But in all this we must remember that what we are currently talking about, whether we call it paradise or heaven, is still part of the intermediate state. As such we should refer to this as the present heaven, to distinguish it from the final heaven. There is still more to come. The present heaven is not our ultimate destiny. Yes, we 'die and go to heaven' in that we 'go to be with the Lord' and that will be heavenly! Paradise even! But that is still not our eternal home.

Most Christians think only of a spiritualised up-in-the-clouds heaven, such as described at the start of this chapter. This needs challenging. We cannot ignore Jesus' return and the new creation to come. This is where we will spend eternity. When in John 14:2 Jesus mentioned preparing a place for us, a home within the Father's house, he was referring to a temporary dwelling place and an eventual move elsewhere. The present heaven is a stopover, not a final destination. For this, we must read on to the very end of the Bible where we will find a new heaven and a new earth. We will focus on this in our next chapter.

Chapter Twenty-Three

A New Heaven and a New Earth

In the previous chapter we looked at what we might mean by 'heaven' and ended by saying that we need to distinguish between what we might call the present heaven and that which is to come, namely a new heaven and a new earth. It is this new creation which forms the final destination for those who belong to Christ but this is not often taught. As we come towards the end of this book, it is not only appropriate but also essential to rectify this omission and spend time learning what we can about our amazing future.

It is a common belief that when we die we 'go to heaven', or at least that is our hope. But so often this heaven is regarded as a rather ethereal other-worldly state of existence with not much to attract us if we don't fancy floating around on clouds or playing the harp, with perhaps a bit of halo polishing to fill in the time. And the thought of it being like an endless church service with a mega playlist of songs is not that appealing either. All of this is part of a myth that has grown up around certain assumptions and misunderstandings which make us automatically think of heaven in these terms. Such imagery has also been bolstered by many Christian songs and hymns, as well as pieces of art. The end result is confusion about our eternal future.

People are generally taught (or led to suppose) that heaven must be a purely spiritual place. If it were physical in any way then this would make it less special or less sacred. God is spirit so heaven is spiritual. In all this we have tended to follow the approach of Greek thinking with its dualistic division of reality into two distinct components, the higher spiritual realm and the lower material world which are always in opposition to each other. Death liberates us from the confines of any kind of material world, and allows us to join the entirely spiritual joys of paradise. Any kind of physicality in the afterlife is simply not permitted as it cannot be beneficial. So although we may read about a heavenly city, with its streets, trees, water, fruit and the like, these can only be mere symbols. This is figurative language only.

An afterlife that was only spiritual came into Christian thinking quite early in its history and then developed in later centuries through the influence of the Neoplatonists. We have mentioned them before in Chapter Seven. To recap, the Neoplatonists were steeped in the earlier teaching of Plato (428–348 BC) whose dualism had divided reality into a higher spiritual world of perfect ideals, or Forms, and a lower world of their physical appearance in our earthly lives.

Basically, Neoplatonists fused the ideas of Plato with Christian teaching, and so created a new religious system. However, becoming a Christian means we should no longer allow ourselves to be conformed to the patterns of this world's thinking. Instead we should be transformed by the renewing of our mind (see Rom. 12:2). But when Neoplatonists became Christians they did not leave behind their existing Greek-based Platonic belief system but instead used it as a lens through which to interpret the scriptures and Christian teaching in general. One consequence was that the allegorical method of interpreting scripture came to rule church theology, an approach which undercuts much of the Bible's revelation, including that of an eternal future for humanity in which the physical and the spiritual coexist in perfect harmony. The result was therefore a different understanding of the afterlife than that found in the Bible.

So what about the common view that as believers in Christ we 'die and go to heaven'? This is correct provided we distinguish between the present heaven, a temporary place for our spirits while we await our new bodies, and the final or ultimate heaven which will be our permanent home for all eternity.

When believers in Christ die they go to be with Jesus, what Paul describes as being 'at home with the Lord' (2 Cor. 5:8). Jesus is now in heaven, or paradise, as we described in our previous chapter, and so being with him is indeed being in heaven, or at least in a heavenly state. Even if this is not where we will live forever, it is still a place of perfect joy and peace. But it also incorporates anticipation, as there is even more to look forward to once we have been resurrected and become part of the new heaven and the new earth.

So the first part of our life after death is indeed heavenly, but it is still only an intermediate stage. This is 'end of life' heaven, not 'end of the age' heaven. At the end of the age, we will live in a renewed cosmos which will be even more exciting than our temporary home, and a more relevant message to preach now than that of a disembodied existence in an ethereal heaven which goes on for ever.

But before we look in more detail at what the Bible tells us about the new heaven and the new earth, we ought to mention another aspect of the intermediate stage, what is known as the Millennium. This topic requires more consideration than we can give it here, but in brief we can say this is the period which immediately precedes the new heaven and new earth, during which Jesus is reigning on the old earth, having returned in bodily form. It is usually understood that his saints have returned with him, having now also been resurrected so that they can also participate in his reign in some way. Details of this are often disputed and certainly it will be a strange time on earth as history comes to a climax and the current age draws to a close. The main verses about the Millennium are in Revelation 20:1-6, but this is not a totally original idea as it represents the fulfilment of the messianic age promised through the prophets in the Hebrew scriptures. What is additional in Revelation chapter 20 is that a particular length of time is now stated, namely 1,000 years, hence the term 'millennium'. To be fair, in a book like Revelation numbers may be more symbolic than literal. In this case, a thousand years may simply denote a very long period but this does not overrule the overall idea of a Millennium. It does, however, indicate that the Millennium is also temporary. It will come to an end. It is not the final state, just a prelude to it.

As we turn to the new heaven and the new earth mentioned in Revelation chapters 21 and 22 we comment first on the terminology. Frequently in scripture the words 'heaven' and 'earth' are linked together into a single phrase to signify the whole of creation (as in Gen. 1:1). Hebrew has no specific word for 'universe' so the phrase 'heaven and earth' is used to refer to the entire cosmos, consisting of the earth, the sky and outer space. Likewise to talk about a 'new heaven and new earth' means the recreation of an entirely new cosmos, a new earth with its own atmosphere and space beyond.

We should also note that the phrase 'new heavens and a new earth' has already occurred in the Old Testament, in Isaiah 65:17 and 66:22. There are no details here about what these will be like, simply that God will create them and that once he has made them they will endure before him. Some believe these verses could still be referring to the Millennium, or the messianic age, but the use of the word 'new' suggests otherwise, and the fact that they will endure indicates this is not something temporary like the Millennium.

There are certain verses in both testaments of the Bible which make it clear that one day the existing creation will 'pass away' but which don't give any indication of what may come next. For instance, Psalm 102:26 states that the earth and the heavens will perish and will all wear out like a garment and eventually be discarded. In similar vein Isaiah proclaims that 'the heavens will vanish like smoke, the earth will wear out like a garment' (Isa. 51:6). As for Jesus, he stated that 'heaven and earth will pass away' when making a comparison with his own words which will never pass away (Matt. 24:35; Luke 21:33). Most dramatic of all is a passage in 2 Peter chapter 3 which declares that on the day of the Lord the 'heavens will disappear with a roar; the elements will be destroyed by fire, and the earth and everything done in it will be laid bare . . . That day will bring about the destruction of the heavens by fire, and the elements will melt in the heat' (2 Pet. 3:10-12). Perhaps Peter had in mind the verse in Isaiah which states that 'all the stars in the sky will be dissolved and the heavens rolled up like a scroll' (Isa. 34:4). Then, on a more positive note, Peter, perhaps still thinking of Isaiah, adds that 'in keeping with his promise we are looking forward to a new heaven and a new earth, where righteousness dwells' (v13).

All this raises many questions. How will God actually do this? Will the existing creation be completely destroyed and replaced by another *ex nihilo* or will this be a radical renewal of what already exists? Scholars are divided on this. Most believe that the language used suggests destroy and replace, a complete disappearance of the old before the appearance of the new. Others advocate a radical change of the existing cosmos rather than a replacement; after all, God said he is making all things new, not making all new things (Rev. 21:5). So it makes sense to start our own exploration of this debate with the meaning of the word 'new' within this context.

The Greek word for new in Revelation 21:5 is based upon *kainos*. The idea behind this word is not new in time, as in the most recent (this would be *neos*), but new as in a different quality or superior in form to that which has gone before. This is also reflected in 2 Corinthians 5:17 where Paul states that if anyone is in Christ that person is a new creation, the old has gone, the new is here. We experience being a new creation and yet remain the same person. We are still who we are but a noticeable transformation has occurred. Similarly with the whole new creation to come. It will not be totally brand new like something never seen before. Rather, it will be recognisable while at the same time it will have been significantly transformed.

As for the imagery of fire in these verses, the two options are that the existing creation will be *consumed* by fire, suggesting absolute destruction in readiness for replacement, or *refined* by fire which might indicate deconstruction followed by restoration and renewal. The verses in 2 Peter chapter 3 may seem to indicate obliteration on a cosmic scale, but perhaps Peter is talking more about a cleansing by fire, a purging of all the old ways, a permanent elimination of sin and all its effects.

The other passages quoted earlier are somewhat ambiguous in this respect. The heavens vanish or are rolled up like a scroll, yet the stars dissolve; creation becomes worn out and discarded; everything simply perishes or passes away. In Revelation 20:11 John talks of the earth and heavens fleeing from God's presence as there is 'no place for them'. It is as though God has no further use for them so he has dismissed them from his presence. There is no mention here of dissolution. In this context, 'passing away' may just mean their present condition disappears to allow for a new version. As such there can also be continuity, a real connection with the past. After all, it is quite possible that God can burn up the bad and refine the good at the same time.

We may be tempted to compare what will happen at the end with the Flood, that previous cataclysmic and devastating event in which the earth was destroyed in order for some kind of renewal to take place. While we cannot actually go back to pre-Flood times to understand what it was like then, clearly the earth and its immediate atmosphere must have undergone a dramatic change while remaining fundamentally what God intended, a home for humanity. This is a valid comparison, providing we realise that purging the earth with water (which God promised he would never do again) had a limited effect. It will take a greater purging by fire to produce an appropriate new home for redeemed humanity.

It is clear the earth cannot remain as it is forever. Equally, we can be sure that earth's redemption is essential to God's plan to redeem and restore the whole of his creation. Meanwhile, creation groans in eager expectation for God's purposes to be fulfilled (see Rom. 8:19ff). Once we as his people are fully redeemed then creation's frustration will be over. Our new home will be ready for us.

Overall, it seems likely that the new creation will be related to the old. The idea of regeneration is more biblical. God doesn't usually wipe everything out and start completely afresh. Moreover, under God's creative power and wisdom it is perfectly possible that the whole may be totally destroyed while the constituent parts are not, and that these can be reconstituted in a new and enduring way. Ultimately, however, once we are part of the new creation we may not care how God produced it. We will be enjoying it too much! Whatever he does, the result will be a fitting home for a new humanity in new bodies. In particular, the new earth will have heavenly qualities. It will embody the heavenliness of heaven through God's presence and glory and the complete execution of his will. It will be all that we expect of heaven but in a material realm.

Inevitably we wonder what it will be like to live in the new heaven and the new earth. Natural curiosity makes us want to speculate on matters such as our gender, age, ethnicity, what we will eat and drink and spend our time doing. How much can we know in advance? Looking around our current world may offer some clues but the realities will always be beyond our current experience.

What we can be certain about is what won't be there. There will be no more tears, death, mourning, crying, pain or suffering, because the old order of things has passed away (see Rev. 21:4). Sin and all its effects will have gone forever, such is the complete and glorious salvation that Christ has won for us.

Above all, rather than speculate on what things might be like, we should rest content in the knowledge that everything will be more wonderful than we can imagine. We can live now in anticipation of the magnificent promise found in 1 Corinthians 2:9 that no eye has seen, no ear has heard, no human mind has conceived what God has prepared for those who love him. Hallelujah!

Chapter Twenty-Four

Caught Up to Heaven

In this book we have been seeking biblical answers to the many difficult questions we face concerning death and what comes afterwards. This means we have steered clear of those who have offered at least some answers from other sources, in particular from their own personal near-death or after-death experiences, during which they claim to have been 'caught up to heaven' or at least to have seen heaven in some way. Such accounts may be told with sincere intentions and even contain some authentic elements, but they need to be evaluated in the light of what we have been learning from the Bible. Caution is required. Discernment is crucial.

We should always remember what Jesus taught in Luke 16:27-31 in the well-known story of the rich man and Lazarus. Suffering in *hades*, the rich man begged that Abraham should send Lazarus back to his father's house to warn his five brothers to avoid this place of torment. Abraham refused, saying, 'They have Moses and the Prophets; let them listen to them.' From this passage we should realise that the first port of call in seeking answers to questions about the afterlife, or in assessing near-death or post-death encounters of any kind, should always be the Word of God. So we will devote this chapter to the examples in the Bible of those who experienced death and came back to life in this world. What can we learn from these?

There are three such cases in the Old Testament, all associated with Elijah and Elisha: the widow of Zarephath's son (1 Kgs 17:17-22), the Shunammite's son (2 Kgs 4:18-37) and the dead body of a man who was thrown into Elisha's grave and came into contact with his bones (2 Kgs 13:20-21). In the New Testament, Jesus raised three people back to life: Jairus' daughter (Luke 8:40-56), the widow of Nain's son (Luke 7:11-17) and Lazarus of Bethany (John 11:38-44). Then in Acts, Peter raised Dorcas (9:36-43) and Eutychus was brought back to life by Paul (20:7-12).

We should also add the strange story of those in Jerusalem whose tombs broke open due to the earthquake which occurred when Jesus was crucified. Matthew records that at this time 'the bodies of many holy people who had died were raised to life' (Matt. 27:52).

Of course, in all the cases mentioned above, they would die again. This was not their final resurrection. They did not come back to life in a new body. But the main point to be made here is that from not a single one of them do we hear anything about their experience in heaven or of the afterlife in general. The Bible is totally silent in all these cases. They must have chatted to their friends and family about what it had been like for them during those few hours or days (indeed we read that the widow of Nain's son did sit up and immediately begin to talk, Luke 7:15) but nothing from their lips is recorded in scripture for us to learn from. This seems significant.

Another important example is Paul, who in 2 Corinthians 12:2-4 writes about his visitation to heaven: 'I know a man in Christ who fourteen years ago was caught up to the third heaven. Whether it was in the body or out of the body I do not know – God knows.' We said in an earlier chapter that the third heaven is the highest heaven, where God dwells, so this was definitely an amazing experience. But Paul adds, this man was 'caught up to paradise and heard inexpressible things, things that no one is permitted to tell'. Paul is adamant that he can say no more about it. He can mention that it happened to him but he cannot pass on anything he had heard there. He even feels he has to distance himself from it now by writing in the third person ('I know a man . . .'). Obviously, he was consciously aware during his visit though he was not sure if at the time he was in his body or out of it. This was an extraordinary episode in his life and we can only wonder why Paul was granted this incredible journey into the heavenly realms, but hopefully it encouraged him to remain faithful and steadfast when back on earth, until he went there again at the end of his life.

A few of the Old Testament prophets also had heavenly visions or visitations. Isaiah saw the throne room of God (Isa. chapter 6), Ezekiel saw heaven opened to him and had visions of God (Ezek. chapter 1), and Daniel also had night visions or dreams which included heaven (Dan. chapter 7). These all had specific purposes. Isaiah underwent cleansing and then was commissioned to speak for God. Ezekiel and Daniel were chosen to bring prophetic words into their current situation or about the future. All of these seem to have had the intention that as servants of God they could minister more effectively, not so that they could boast or regard themselves as special. Moreover, we can say that their experiences were designed to bring significant benefits for others, both in their own time and for us now, as through these we can learn much more about the majesty and holiness of God, his throne room and the judgements he makes.

Finally, there is the best-known New Testament example of heavenly visions and visitations, namely that of John in the book of Revelation. John was physically on Patmos but four times we are told he was in the Spirit, meaning that the Holy Spirit took his spirit into another realm (1:10, 4:2, 17:3, 21:20). In particular, John saw a door standing open in heaven and was invited to 'come up here' (4:1). As well as looking round heaven John also saw into the future, including the new heaven and earth which we mentioned in the last chapter. Only the Holy Spirit could do this for someone before they had died.

Moreover, we should note that at the beginning of the book of Revelation Jesus gave permission for John to write all this down. In fact he instructed him to do so (1:19; see also 21:5). There was just one small exception when John was told specifically not to write something down (10:4). So what is recorded in the book of Revelation comes with the highest authority, that of Jesus himself. In particular we are warned that adding or taking away anything from what is contained within the book will have serious consequences.

We are nearly at the end of our biblical exploration of the many different topics and themes concerning death and what comes after. We will conclude by summarising some of the main points.

Chapter Twenty-Five

In Conclusion

We are coming to the end of our journey in which we have been seeking biblical answers to the many demanding and often uncomfortable questions we face concerning death and what comes afterwards. To what extent we have been successful in our search may be debated, but hopefully we have kept to our commitment to discover such answers from the biblical texts because it is only through the revelation contained within the Word of God that we can hope to find the truth we need.

The main reason for this book is that we might truly anticipate the afterlife which God has for us. We have a wonderful gospel of salvation by grace through faith and we should ensure that as part of this we preach a correct view of death and what comes afterwards.

In some cases we have been exploring biblical truths long neglected or ignored. In attempting to restore them we have been aiming to show what the Bible has said all along but which we have failed to grasp. During the course of our studies we have tried to remove certain wrong ideas, especially those from Greek-based thinking, and to stress that as well as an afterlife in the present heaven, there is even more in the eternal state.

It was important to start with a correct view of the nature of Man as created by God. The bipartite approach (body and soul/spirit) seemed the most appropriate way to think of human beings, but a tripartite view (body, soul and spirit) does not undermine our later discussions and conclusions, and so was not dismissed completely.

What ought to be dismissed without reservation are the ideas of soul sleep, a timeless eternity, purgatory, communicating with the dead and a second chance of salvation after death. Equally, we should not entertain the idea that animals have souls like ours. They do not 'go to heaven' or have an afterlife as such, but we can look forward to enjoying newly created animals in the new heaven and new earth.

We should also be sceptical of any claims about the innocence of babies and hence their automatic entry into heaven and a guaranteed afterlife. In this matter, as in many others, we rely upon God's love and justice, and that he will fulfil the desires of his own heart. We also cautioned against many of the modern views of heaven and hell which are contrary to what God has revealed.

It is to be hoped that all these discussions have been profitable to some extent, even if certain disagreements remain.

As we come to the end of our survey of the afterlife let's remind ourselves of something we said at the start and on which everyone can agree. We all suffer from a terminal disease. The death rate is 100 per cent. Our mortality is obvious from early in life and keeps coming at us like an unstoppable train. It is how we cope with this that matters. Recognising our own mortality can give us an incentive to make the most of our time now, to make each day count. In addition, it can unfasten us from this life and reset our mind on what is to come before it is too late. Most people seemingly live unprepared for death. Some are given a chance to get themselves ready, but for others death can be sudden and unexpected. So it is not morbid to focus in advance on death; it is wise.

For Christians, death may be an interruption, even an enemy, but not a great disaster. It is an instant of change but not the end of everything. We can, and should, live in anticipation rather than anxiety. Meditating on the future life can help and is something we should do regularly. As David said in one of his psalms, 'Show me, LORD, my life's end and the number of my days; let me know how fleeting my life is' (Ps. 39:4).

As humans, we often have a strong sense we are created for more than just a temporary span in this world. Although we may prefer to keep hidden our feelings about our own mortality, we do generally seek answers about the afterlife. Is death really the end of our existence or is there something, anything, to come? This book has been an attempt to address this. Not everything in it may be totally satisfactory, but it is hoped that much will be helpful. It has certainly been a challenge to work through some of these issues myself but also beneficial to have had the chance to think more about them.

There will come a time when heaven and earth will be unified in a way that is not possible now. The gap between them will have gone. But only when God's will is fully done in both heaven and earth. At present there are lots of competing human wills operating on the current earth. This is why there is not yet heaven on earth and why we have to keep praying 'your will be done on earth as it is in heaven' (Matt. 6:10). But one day that prayer will no longer be needed, the sovereign will of God becomes the only one in operation.

Is this what you are looking forward to? Is this what you are anticipating when you think about life after death?

We finish with one of John's great statements from the end of the book of Revelation: 'Look! God's dwelling-place is now among the people, and he will dwell with them. They will be his people, and God himself will be with them and be their God' (Rev. 21:3).

Amen!

Scripture Index

Genesis

Leviticus

Numbers

Deuteronomy

Joshua

1 Samuel

2 Samuel

1 Kings

2 Kings

1 Chronicles

2 Chronicles

Job

Psalms

Proverbs

Ecclesiastes

Mark

Luke

John

Acts

Romans

1 Corinthians

2 Corinthians

Galatians

Ephesians

Philippians

Colossians

1 Thessalonians

2 Thessalonians

1 Timothy

2 Timothy

Hebrews

2 Maccabees

www.ingramcontent.com/pod-product-compliance
Lightning Source LLC
LaVergne TN
LVHW020042110826
845155LV00029B/603

* 9 7 8 1 9 1 7 4 5 5 6 1 9 *